John H. Wynne, Samuel Wale

Choice Emblems

Natural, historical, fabulous, moral and divine, for the improvement and pastime of youth : ornamented with near fifty handsome allegorical engravings, designed on purpose for this work

John H. Wynne, Samuel Wale

Choice Emblems

Natural, historical, fabulous, moral and divine, for the improvement and pastime of youth : ornamented with near fifty handsome allegorical engravings, designed on purpose for this work

ISBN/EAN: 9783337386542

Printed in Europe, USA, Canada, Australia, Japan

Cover: Foto ©ninafisch / pixelio.de

More available books at **www.hansebooks.com**

CHOICE EMBLEMS,

NATURAL, HISTORICAL, FABULOUS,
MORAL AND DIVINE,

FOR THE IMPROVEMENT AND PASTIME OF

YOUTH.

ORNAMENTED WITH
Near Fifty Handsome Allegorical ENGRAVINGS,
Designed on purpose for this Work.

With pleasing and familiar DESCRIPTIONS to each,
in Prose and Verse,

Serving to display the BEAUTIES and MORALS of
the ANCIENT FABULISTS.

The whole calculated to convey the golden Lessons
of Instruction under a new and more delightful
Dress.

WRITTEN FOR THE AMUSEMENT OF
The Right Honourable Lord NEWBATTLE.

" *Say, should the philosophic mind disdain*
" *That good, which makes each humbler bosom vain?*
" *Let school-taught pride dissemble all it can,*
" *These little things are great to little man.*"
Goldsmith.

LONDON:
PRINTED FOR GEORGE RILEY, IN CURZON
STREET, MAY FAIR.

MD,CC,LXXII.

TO THE

RIGHT HONOURABLE

Lady ELIZABETH KERR,

ELDEST DAUGHTER OF

The Rt. Hon. Lord ANCRAM,

MADAM,

YOUR ladyship will immediately perceive, that the author of the subsequent allegories, has availed himself of the honour of your permission to this dedication.

So gracious a condescension is still the more pleasing to him, as it gives a peculiar propriety to the address of this publication. —Elevated by nobility and patronised by innocence, while it aims to recommend religion, morality, and all the Virtues.

Naturalists, my lady, acquaint us, that the Rose in its infant state, while in its bud contains, in epitome, all the native sweetness, bloom and beauty of maturity :—Those who best know your ladyship, can never accuse me of flattery, while I presume to to prophecy, from the evidence of your difpofition, that the latent hereditary ornaments of your illuftrious family will in you, one day fhine out with fuperior brightnefs, and juftly entitle you, not only a blefling to your inferiors, a glory to your fex; but, in a word, a pattern to the nobility, your cotemporaries.

Thefe inftructive emblems, written for the amufement of your noble brother, The Right Honourable the Lord Newbattle, claim a particular attention from your ladyship, as they recommend the immediate paths to happiness both here and hereafter.

Be this Eliza's care, let this,
Her earliest thoughts engage,
Be this the business of her youth,
And comfort of her age.

Attentive then, consult the muse,
And each fair path pursue;
Let's mend a world, by precept I,
And by example You.

Your Ladyship's sincere,

And most obedient

Humble servant,

THE AUTHOR.

INTRODUCTION.

ALL the happiness and glory of a state, says a celebrated writer, depend on the education of youth; and it may be added, there is not a more important duty incumbent on a parent than the early cultivation of their tender offspring----However little the following trifles may appear on the first view, it is humbly presumed, that, on their perusal, they will be found to contribute somewhat towards that great and desirable end. ---The author of the following sheets has taken Nature for his principle guide and it has been his sole aim, to describe her in the purest forms; in which he has it not so much at heart to be considered as an elegant poet, as to be approved for a good moralist.

Fable has already employed many learned and ingenious pens, both ancient and modern, and as the emblematical hieroglyphic devices of the Hebrews, Egyptians and other ancients seem to afford fit subjects for instruction, it has been the Author's endeavour to send many of these into the world under a modern habit--and if some of them are found to be too puerile for the learned eye, it must be remembered, that such were written for the amusement of a young nobleman not more than nine years old.———Yet,

" ———*Is not the earth*
" *With various living* creatures *and the air*
" *Replenished?---They also know,*
" *And reason not contemptibly:*"

For many of the brute creatures seem so formed by instinct, as to make up an universal satire on mankind---For where is the undutiful child but must be ashamed to see himself outdone by the stork in filial duty and affection? the faithless servant by the fidelity

of

of the dog, the sluggard by the lark, or the man of indolence by the bee and woodpecker?---The false friend, the inconstant lover may here find proper lessons to copy from. In fine, there are scarcely any persons in life who will not find somewhat here which may suit their particular situations, or inculcate in their minds the most necessary virtues. If this great end be attained, the purpose of the Author is fully answered; if not, he can only lament the ill fortune of his endeavours, but trusts, he shall ever be happy in the integrity of his good intentions.

CONTENTS.

Emb.		Page
I.	A Young Stork carrying his old Parent on his Back - -	1
II.	Harpocrates the God of Silence	5
III.	A Boy and Bee-hive --	9
IV.	A Dog lying Dead at his Master's Sepulchre - - -	13
V.	The Senfitive Plant - -	17
VI.	The Bat flying from the rifing Sun	21
VII.	A Turtle Dove bemoaning its Mate	25
VIII.	Hope - - - -	29
IX.	The Sun-Flower --	33
X.	A Crown of Gold and a Crown of Thorns lying together - -	7
XI.		

Emb.	Page
XI. Castor and Pollux	41
XII. A Sun-Dial	45
XIII. A Queen and Shepherd's Boy	49
XIV. Pallas armed	53
XV. Fortune, with her Wheel	57
XVI. A Bee upon a Rose	61
XVII. The Crocodile and Traveller	65
XVIII. A Moth flying round a Candle	69
XIX. Diogenes	73
XX. A wounded Stag	77
XXI. A Vine supported, and another creeping on the Ground	81
XXII. Apollo killing the Serpent Python	85
XXIII. A Rock in the midst of a stormy Sea	89
XXIV. The Traveller and Snake	93
XXV. A Fish caught by an Angler	97
XXVI. The Return of the Argonauts	101
XXVII. A Boy and Butterfly	105
XXVIII. An Eagle chained to a Log	109
XXIX. Leucothöe buried alive	113
XXX. A Hog lying Dead in a Garden	117
XXXI. A Chariot driven violently down a Precipice	121
XXXII. The Moon in the Increase	125

XXXIII. A

Emb.	Page
XXXIII. A Bird caught by a Fowler	129
XXXIV. A Lion viewing himself in the Water	133
XXXV. Apollo and Daphne	137
XXXVI. A Rose among Thorns	141
XXXVII. Time	145
XXXVIII. The Woodpecker	149
XXXIX. A Boy and Bird's Nest	153
XL. The Peacock	157
XLI. Fame	161
XLII. An Eagle and Serpent	165
XLIII. Narcissus admiring himself in a Fountain	169
XLIV. An Oak struck with Lightning	173
XLV. A Pelican feeding its Young	177
XLVI. The Tulip and Myrtle	181
XLVII. A Pyramid overturned	185

CHOICE
EMBLEMS.

EMBLEM I.
Of FILIAL DUTY AND AFFECTION.

SEE the young STORK his duteous wing
  prepare,
His aged Sire to feed with conſtant care;
O'er hills and dales his precious load conveys,
And the great debt of filial duty pays,
Grateful return! by Nature's ſelf deſign'd,
A fair example ſet to human kind.

Should'ſt thou refuſe thy parents needful aid,
The very Stork might the foul crime upbraid:
Be mindful how they rear'd thy tender youth,
Bear with their frailties; ſerve them ſtill with
  truth,
So may'ſt thou with long life and peace be bleſt,
'Till Heaven ſhall call thee to eternal reſt.

THIS bird is generally esteemed an emblem of filial love, in so much that it has ever acquired the name of *pious* from the just regard it is said to pay to acts of filial piety and duty.

Storks live to a very advanced age; the consequence of which is, that their limbs grow feeble, their feathers fall off, and they are no ways capable of providing for their own food or safety. Being birds of passage, they are under another inconvenience also, which is, that they are not able to remove themselves from one country to another at the usual season. In all these circumstances, it is reported that their young ones assist them, covering them with their wings and nourishing them with the warmth of their bodies, even bringing them provisions in their beaks, and carrying them from place to place on their backs, or supporting them with their wings; in this manner returning, as much as lies in their power, the care which was bestowed on them when they were young ones in the nest. A striking example, of filial piety inspired by Instinct; from which Reason itself needs not be ashamed to take example.

"HONOUR thy father and thy mother, that thy days may be long in the land which the Lord thy God giveth thee" was an expreſs commandment, and the only one to which a promiſe was annexed.—And among the Iſraelites the ſlighteſt offence againſt a parent was puniſhed in the moſt exemplary manner.

Certainly nothing can be more juſt or reaſonable than that we ſhould love, honour, and ſuccour thoſe who are the very authors of our being, and to whoſe tender cares (under Heaven) we owe the continuance of it during the helpleſs ſtate of our infancy.

Love, charity, and an intercourſe of good offices, are what undoubtedly we owe to al mankind, and he who omits them is guilty of ſuch a crime as generally carries its puniſhment along with it;—but to our parents more, much more than all this is due; and when we are ſerving them we ought to reflect that whatever difficulties we go through for their ſakes, we cannot do more for them than they have done for us, and that there is no danger

danger of our over-paying the vaſt debt of gratitude they have laid us under.

In fine, we ſhould conſider that it is a duty moſt peculiarly inſiſted on by Heaven itſelf, and if we obey the command, there is no doubt but we ſhall alſo receive the reward annexed to it.

EMBLEM

(5)

EMBLEM II.

OF SILENCE.

LO here the portrait of that ancient pow'r
Which sway'd before the world's great natal hour,
SILENCE! the still companion of the wise
That shrouds ev'n Folly in its deep disguise:
" A living death that is of nothing made,
" In noon day's sun wrapp'd up in thickest shade,
Blush not, good youth to court his friendly aid;
He shall your secrets keep, your friends retain,
Improve your honour and secure your gain.

Be not too rash in speech, lest others find
The depth and secrets of your inmost mind:
Silence may oft times make your sense extoll'd,
But the word spoke can never be recall'd.

B 3   SILENCE

SILENCE was a quality fo much rever'd among fome of the ancients, that their priests and philofophers tried their initiates and difciples by enjoining them taciturnity for a certain ftated period, teaching it as the firft of all fciences.

They likewife paid divine honours to Silence, worfhipping it as a deity, under the name of Harpocrates, who was reprefented as in the emblem, and whofe figure was fufficiently expreffive of the moral they meant to inculcate.

It is a fure friend in difficulties; it is a charm againft anger, and a kind of talifman which generally gains its owner a knowledge of the thoughts of others, while it leaves him entirely mafter of his own. Though it is ufeful to thofe of weak parts, yet need not the wife be afhamed of it. In effect, it has this beft of qualities, that it may do much good, but is entirely incapable of harm.

A S

AS a vain babbler is generally the most ridiculous of mankind; so Silence is mostly a sign of wisdom; for if it should even sometimes happen that the silent man is a person of mean talents, yet it must be allowed at least, to be one mark of his sagacity, that he can devise the means to cover and conceal from others his want of abilities.

When a man is justly rebuked, Silence is often better than a laboured defence, as it is generally the true token of an ingenuous mind.— And even when one is reproached unjustly, how glorious is it to be silent and answer only by one's actions!

" How beautiful is a word in due season!" says the wise man; but he who is perpetually talking is not likely to reap such a praise because he minds no season; whereas one that knows how to keep silence may easily know also by his observations on the discourse of others when to speak; and his words being few,

few, are likely to be the more properly applied, and will be the more esteemed by the hearers. ---But in a multitude of words, there is often a multitude of errors, and to rule that little member, the Tongue, is often more difficult than to govern a city.

EMBLEM

EMBLEM III.

Of the Danger of Pleasures.

BEHOLD the boy, forbidden sweets to prove,
With luckless hand the honey'd hive remove,
Straight with an angry hum that sounds to arms,
Forth rush the winged tribe, in all their swarms,
Too late, alas! they make th' offender find,
That pleasure's honey leaves a sting behind.

Learn hence ye heedless train, who gaily glide
In youth's trim bark down life's uncertain tide,
That death oft lurks beneath some gilded toy,
And poison mingles in the cup of joy.

THE thoughtless child overturns the hive, in order to get at the honey; he knows that the bees have sweets, but he forgets that they have also stings. When he has done the mischief, he perceives it too late; for the industrious people shew him that they will not be so disturbed with impunity, and he finds it impossible to get the honey unless he were able to destroy those who guarded it.

Amazed at the consequences of his action, he flies with precipitation; but is overtaken by the insects who settling upon him, leave behind them their stings, the anguish of which may serve as a perpetual memorial of his rashness, and warn him how he attempts stolen sweets for the future.

IN many people of a more mature age we see this emblem verified; and though common experience might prevent the evil yet so careless are some that they will make use of no experience but their own, which is always dearly bought, and

and may sometimes come too late to have the effect desired by every rational and thinking person.

The wild and unthinking always imagine *stolen waters* to be sweet, and *hidden bread* to be pleasant; and, proceeding on this maxim they often plunge themselves into the most ruinous circumstances, and repent only when it is too late to amend them.

The misfortune is, that they go on without consideration, and when they find themselves attacked by evils they cry out " *Who would have thought it?*" when in reality they themselves might have determined upon the event, if they had thought at all, or believed the counsel of those who wished to promote their welfare.

But they will overturn the hive, they must have the honey; while they little expect the sting;---when they feel it (like the boy in the emblem,) surprize is added to their affliction, and their distress is doubled by their being no ways provided to sustain the accident.

If

If you would be wife, take not the honey while the hive is swarming, let not your pleasures be mixed with guilt, and then you may rest secure, that they will leave no sting behind them.

EMBLEM.

EMBLEM IV.

Of Fidelity.

BEHOLD the faithful beaſt, reſolv'd to die
Near where his much lov'd maſter's aſhes lie,
Emblem of conſtancy, he yields his breath
For ancient love, and keeps his faith by death.

Hence learn Fidelity;---with grateful mind,
Repay the courteous; to your friends be kind:
Whatever fortune on your life attend,
The beſt of treaſures is a faithful friend.

THE Dog is of all animals the moſt faithful, as well as the moſt ſagacious. There are few things which a good dog may not be trained up to do to ſerve his maſter, and if he be well uſed there are fewer ſtill that he will not do to defend him.

We have many inſtances, both in ancient and modern ſtory, of the fidelity of theſe creatures and ſome of their having been the cauſe of diſcovering their maſter's murder by obſtinately refuſing to ſtir from his corpſe. Often have they ſaved men's lives by interpoſing againſt thoſe who offered them violence, and have proved an uſeful and a faithful guard both to their perſons and their properties.

Homer tells us, that after Troy was deſtroyed by the Grecians, Ulyſſes returning from the ſiege in mean apparel having gone through various dangers, and been abſent in all twenty years, was unknown to his queen, and every perſon in his palace, but his dog recognized him.

---Forgot

——Forgot by all his own domestic crew,
The faithful dog alone his master knew,
Unfed, unhous'd, neglected, on the clay,
Like an old servant now cashier'd he lay,
Touch'd with resentment to ungrateful man,
And longing to behold his ancient lord again:
Him when he saw, he rose and crawl'd to meet,
('Twas all he could) and fawn'd and lick'd his feet,
Seiz'd with dumb joy---Then falling by his side,
Own'd his returning lord, look'd up, and died.

GRATITUDE and fidelity to our friends are the best qualities that can adorn our nature: The emblem of the dog is a very striking one, in this regard, and is calculated to convey the severest satire on false friends and ungrateful persons.

There is nothing in which a man should be more cautious and deliberate than in his choice

choice of a friend, but having once chosen him, he should repose in him all manner of confidence, and in his turn keep his secrets, and be ever ready to do him any manner of service that is consistent with the rules of religion and virtue; he that requires any thing contrary to these can never be a true friend; for that is properly speaking no friendship which is not founded upon a virtuous basis; it is only a connexion of interest, which the first puff of adverse fortune will blow away, and scatter to the winds of heaven.

But when you have really gotten a true friend,

"Grapple him to your soul with hooks of steel"

Abide by him alike in prosperity and in adversity, and let no change of circumstances change your regards or services;---so may you expect assistance in the time of your distress and a comforter in the day of trouble.

EMBLEM.

EMBLEM V.

OF PURITY.

SO nicely form'd by nature's hidden laws,
   Lo! from the touch the confcious plant withdraws.
Emblem of purity; which ſtill retires
From the rude glowing of unhallow'd fires;
Yet ſtill more weak the frequent touch it tries,
Droops in approaching, and by preſſure dies.

   Shun evil's firſt advance; be timely wife,
Shrink at th' *appearance*; fly the *name* of vice
Like this fair plant th' empoiſon'd touch avoid,
Nor be by too much confidence deſtroy'd:
Stand not in your own ſtrength, for 'tis moſt ſure
That ills are eaſier to prevent than cure.

                           THE

THE Senfitive Plant is fo conftructed by Nature that it fhrinks from the warmth of the human touch--A property fo extraordinary for which various caufes are affigned by philofophers occafioned fome ftrange ftories to be told of this wonderful vegetable, one of which was that it would not bear the touch of any but chafte perfons; however the truth is, that it retires alike from the approach of any hand, as has been often experienced.---Among fome papers of a late celebrated poet, there is a fable concerning it, on the plan of that of Apollo and Daphne in Ovid.---He relates that a certain nymph flying from the embraces of Pan the God of the woods, juft as he was on the point of overtaking her was changed into this plant, and ftill retained, in a vegetable, the fame nice chaftity for which fhe had been celebrated when a nymph---The ftory is pretty, and the metamorphofis aptly turned. This Senfitive plant is to be found in the gardens of the curious, and is generally much efteemed by thofe who delight in enquiries into the nature of the vegetable world:---
But

But it is not allowed to be often handled because frequent touching hurts its delicate texture and in time it is supposed would quite destroy it.

IN this vegetable we may see the symbol of a truly virtuous person, who shuns even the shadow of evil, and starts at the thoughts of vice---Those who stand in their own strength can never be sure that they shall not fall; and no distance can be too far to be removed from the habitations of the wicked.

" Vice to avoid" is virtue's earliest rule,
Wisdom's first precept " Not to be a fool."

To become familiar with the name of vice is the first introduction to the practice of it, and to see ill actions unmoved is the first step towards commiting them.

It is thus that people have been led by degrees into the perpretation of crimes at one time, which at another they would have shuddered but to think on; and then have looked back with surprize upon their altered state, and that lost innocence which they never could possess again.

Accustom yourself therefore to shrink like the plant in the emblem whenever vice approaches you. Prevent evil in its first stage, and you will save yourself many periods of unhappiness. Assume a habit of virtue, and it will grow every day easier to you, so may you be enabled to resist temptation; for be assured you can never boast the least degree of freedom from any sin till you shudder at the least shadow of an incitement to commit it.

EMBLEM

EMBLEM VI.

Of Guilt.

SEE where, with drowsy wing, the bird
    of night
Bends from the rising sun, her sullen flight:
Opprefs'd and weaken'd by the morning ray,
She seeks in shades to slumber out the day:
While the blithe Lark ascending chears the
    eye,
Sings as he mounts, and seeks the distant sky.

  Thus conscious Guilt its head detested hides,
Nor Heav'n's, nor man's, nor day's broad
    eye abides;
While virtue still undaunted and serene,
With chearful brow, in open light is seen.

THE

THE BAT is a bird so much accustomed to darkness that it generally flies only by night, and if at any time it is found abroad in the day, impelling it towards the sun, to which it has a particular aversion, is a sure method of surprizing and taking it.

This creature partakes partly of the nature of a beast and partly of that of a bird, its body being formed somewhat like that of a mouse, though it has wings wherewith it mounts in the air; but its flight is always sluggish and heavy, and its whole form is frightfully disagreeable.

THAT the BAT which in its first creation was formed a bird of night, should shun the sun shine, is by no means to be wondered at. It follows its nature, and consequently fulfils in every point the end for which it was made.

Yet how much more do we admire the sprightly Lark who with his morning song awakes the day, and soars towards heaven upon expanded wing!

Would

Would you apply the emblem? In the Lark behold the chearful openness of the virtuous and pious man, who is always found in the fair face of day, and (while the drunkard is retiring to his bed) is seen early risen to salute the day, and after the due tribute rendered to the Being who preserved him through the perils of darkness, he goes chearfully about his temporal concerns, and never seeks the shade but when repose invites him to it.

Such is not the practice of the guilty man: He is ever fond of lurking in the dark, and striving to cover his evil actions with the sable veil of night, because they will not bear the test of open day.

He loves darkness better than light, because his deeds are evil.

When the Bat and the Owl fly, then he goes abroad: He accomplishes his ill actions when there is none to detect him. He returns in the morning;--from the works of darkness; then he hides himself, and says, who shall discover me?

Yet

Yet there is ONE who sees in secret; He shall reward his evil openly: the punishment of his sins shall be upon him; and when his deeds shall be revealed, he shall have no part in the Kingdom of Light.

EMBLEM

EMBLEM VII.

Of Constant Affection.

WITH plaintive cooings, lo! the turtle dove
Laments the fate of his departed love,
His mate, once loſt, no comfort now he knows,
His little breaſt with inward anguiſh glows,
Nor lawns nor groves his throbbing heart can charm
Nor other love his languid boſom warm;
Oppreſs'd with grief, he yields his lateſt breath,
And proves, at laſt his conſtancy in death.

A proper leſſon to the fickle mind,
An emblem apt of tenderneſs refin'd,
Affection pure and undiſſembled love,
Which abſence, time nor death can e'er remove.

THE dove is the gentleſt and moſt loving of birds---for which qualities the ancient heathens feigned that the chariot of Venus the goddeſs of love, was drawn by turtle doves. The conſtancy of the dove is ſuch, that it is become a proverb, and when one of a pair of turtles dies, the other generally pines itſelf to death. So true is their love and ſo far are they from a deſire of changing.——

A remarkable inſtance of the power of inſtinct, and an example worthy of our imitation.

———————

THE dove and lamb are ſo remarkable for their gentleneſs, that they have been adopted as ſymbols of our moſt holy religion, and are always repreſented in the ſacred writings as the moſt perfect emblems of virtue and of innocence.

Conſtancy

Constancy, whether in love or friendship, is certainly one of the most striking proofs of a great and noble mind, as fickleness is of the contrary: Love is but a more refined, a more tender friendship, and when that love is strengthened by the more sacred ties of marriage it ought to be equally lasting and inviolate.

In such a state, the joy or grief of either party must be shared by the other; they must be both as one, or happiness can never be expected.

And to promote this agreeing will, constancy, tenderness, and an allowance for the frailties of humanity, are indispensably necessary.---Where these are united there may be truly said to be an union of souls, which is the greatest felicity on earth.

The emblem of the dove is one of those lessons drawn from nature, whereby the best among us may profit; since we may well be ashamed to be outdone either in constancy or tenderness by any of the brute creation.

    Then like the dove, let constancy and truth,
    And spotless innocence adorn your youth,
    In ev'ry state the same bless'd temper prove,
    Be fix'd in friendship, and be true to love.

EMBLEM

EMBLEM VIII.

Of Necessary Confidence.

HOPE is the firſt great bleſſing here below,
The only balm that heals corroding woe:
It is the ſtaff of age, the ſick man's health,
The priſ'ner's freedom, and the poor man's wealth;
The ſailor's ſafety; laſting as our breath,
It ſtill holds on nor quits us e'en in death.

Encourage Hope which heals all human care
The laſt mad folly is a ſad deſpair.
If you are wiſe the dreadful fiend avoid,
Nor be for want of Heav'n's beſt gift deſtroy'd.

ALAS!

IT is said, in the old heathen fable, that when Prometheus had ſtolen fire from heaven, with which he animated mortal bodies, Jupiter, in anger to mankind, gave Pandora a box which was cloſe ſhut, but which her curioſity (as the God foreſaw) prompting her to open, out flew a variety of plagues and evils, which immediately diſperſed themſelves over the world.---Confounded and aſtoniſhed, Pandora at length ſhut the fatal box again, when all the reſt of its contents being fled, Hope alone remained at the bottom, which proved the only conſolation to mankind for the plagues that Jove had ſent amongſt them.

Hope, according to our ſyſtem is deemed one of the chriſtian virtues, is repreſented as in the Emblem, leaning upon an anchor, whereby is aptly expreſſed her ſteadineſs and truſt---In religious pictures ſhe is moreover generally painted with her eyes turned up towards Heaven. in token of her confidence in that help which comes only from above, and which

which is indeed the only sure aid to trust to, when man forsakes us, and when the storms of this world beat hard upon our bark and threaten to wreck it.

———

ALAS! without Hope, of what value would our mortal existence prove? How should we be enabled to bear up under afflictions, what cordial should we have to oppose to the thousand heart-corroding cares which this frail life abounds with!

It is then we avail ourselves of this anchor, and of the three christian graces, are most relieved by Hope, which leads on, through Faith, to the promise of happier days here, or a better state hereafter.

To be without Hope would be the most dreadful of all earthly punishments: It is the refuge of the poor and needy, and renders the distribution of the lots of men below more equal. Since the high and low, the rich and poor cannot with justice be deemed so widely

diffe-

different in their eſtates, when we conſider that

"Theſe are placed in Hope and thoſe in fear."

Hope is, in ſhort, our beſt companion here below, which leads us as it were by the hand through the midſt of all difficulties and dangers; and it may juſtly be ſaid of it that it is

"The cordial drop Heav'n in our cup has thrown,
"To make the nauſeous draught of life go down.

EMBLEM

EMBLEM IX.

Of Zeal towards God.

TO the all-chearing sun's enlivening rays
  The grateful plant its op'ning leaves displays,
Rejoicing in his beams and radiance bright
Expands and opens with approaching light;
But when dim night extends her dusky shade
Its closing beauties sicken all and fade!
The flow'r which Phœbus' warmth first bade to rise
Lives in his beams, and in his absence dies.

  Each human breast may this example move
To acts of gratitude and heav'nly love
To Him who gives us all our hearts to raise,
Live in his light, and triumph in his praise.

THE Sun-flower was, according to the heathen fable, a nymph called Clytie, who loved and was at first beloved by Phœbus or the sun, and afterwards by him changed into a flower, which ever mindful of the regard she once bore to him always turns itself to his beams---This plant, as it has always been remarked for its property of particularly turning to the sun, so has it likewise been ever esteemed an emblem of gratitude in general, and in particular of that which is owing to God our Creator, in whom we live and move, and have our being, and by whom he is promised the blessings of a future state: a reasonable tribute from mortals for such inestimable benefits!

MAN may learn gratitude from the brutes, and often even from the inanimate part of the creation; and indeed Nature herself does not fail to teach him this lesson, which he must take great pains to eradicate from his heart before he can be so base as to become ungrateful.

Ingratitude

Ingratitude (says the scripture) *is worse than the sin of witch-craft*, and that must be a heinous crime indeed, which is spoken of in such terms in the sacred writings.

He who can return evil for good, or who can even neglect to return a good office, when it is in his power, is so far from ever deserving again to be obliged or assisted, that he does not ever deserve to live.

And if the gratitude we owe to our friends be such an indispensable duty, how much greater is that which we owe to God, to whose paternal care we are indebted for all we are and all we ever shall be!---

How much does it behove us to turn to him as to our sun, in whose beams we live, and whose face being withdrawn, we should return to our primitive nothing.

Remember thy Creator in the days of thy youth, was the precept of a man as wise as he was

was virtuous, and of one who well knew that this was not a fruitless duty, but such an one as would be returned by unnumbered blessings, being showered on the heads of those who attached themselves to it.

" For praise is Heav'n's just due not paid in vain,
" But still return'd in blessings back again
" As dews exhal'd descend in fleecy rain:
" Then, like the flow'r which to the sun displays
" Its orient colours, and invokes his rays
" Still turn your heart to him who reigns above
" Whose yoke is freedom, and whose tribute love!"

EMBLEM

EMBLEM X.

OF THE CARES OF GREATNESS.

LO! where ambition's emblem fit appears,
   That great reward which pays the toil
      of years,
Adorn'd with all the pomp of state, behold,
With jewels blazing rich, the Crown of Gold.
Near, ah! too near, its sure companion lies,
The dire attendant on the dazzling prize,
The Crown of Thorns, whose sharpest stings
      await
On the vain pageantry of regal state.

   Care follows Greatness; guilt or fear annoy
The sceptred prince and all his peace destroy,
And he who to possess a crown is born,
For ev'ry glitt'ring jewel finds a thorn.

AMBITIOUS men can conceive no good or happiness but that which they imagine must arise from greatness; yet he is often the object of their envy who (if the secrets of his heart were known) might more properly be said to deserve their pity.

Of all the pursuits of ambition, a Crown is reckoned the most noble and valuable; and, n the opinion of some men, all human felicity s centred in the circle of it.----But were they exalted to the dignity they covet so much, it is certain they would soon find their error, and be compelled by experience to confess that the Crown of Gold is inseparable from a Crown of Thorns, which is for ever galling the brow of majesty and poisoning all the joys a monarch can expect to taste.

The reflexions which Shakespear puts into the mouth of Prince Henry (afterwards the great Henry V. who conquered the French at Agincourt) are very applicable to this purpose——Seeing the Crown lying on his

father's

father's pillow, he breaks out into the following exclamation.

" Why doth the crown lie there upon his pillow
" Being so troublesome a bed fellow?
" O polish'd perturbation! golden care!
" That keep'st the ports of slumber open wide
" To many a watchful night!—He sleeps with't now;
" Yet not so found, nor half so deeply sweet
" As he whose brow with homely biggen bound,
" Snores out the watch of night---O majesty!
" When thou dost pinch thy bearer, thou dost sit
" Like a rich armour worn in heat of day,
" That scalds with safety.

THAT to be *great* is to be *happy* is one of those errors which have almost at all ages prevailed among the generality of mankind---But that to be *good* is to be *happy* is a secret reserved for the wife and virtuous few, who are the grace

grace and ornament of themselves, their friends, and their country.

An exalted station always brings with it a weight of cares, and he is happier, who in the humble vale of life, pursues his way in the paths of reason and of virtue, than he who shares the favours of a prince or the applauses of a giddy multitude.---

As for a monarch, if he is a tyrant, he must be in perpetual *fears* of his subjects, if a good prince, he must be involved in perpetual *cares* for them : Either way, he stands a chance never to taste of real happiness; and those princes who have gone through the world with the greatest *eclat* have been ready to declare that the Crown of Gold was ever accompanied by one of Thorns and that he who resolves to gratify his *ambition*, must always expect to sacrifice his *happiness*.

EMBLEM

EMBLEM XI.
Of Brotherly Love.

Lo! here the valiant twins, whose glorious name
The Poets confecrate to endless fame!
Two bodies sway'd by one agreeing mind;
Loving in life, and not in death disjoin'd.
For feats of arms through all the world renown'd
For friendship *more*, the brother chiefs were found :---
Thro' life's whole race one common fate they share,
Alike united, or in peace or war,
For Pollux, Castor fights; in battle slain,
Pollux for Castor begs new life in vain,
Yet half his days at length allow'd to give,
Alternately they die, alternate live.

   Learn hence true friendship and fraternal love,
An off'ring grateful to the throne above!

CASTOR

CASTOR and POLLUX are said to have been the sons of Leda, the former being begotten by Tyndarus, was mortal; but the latter being the offspring of Jupiter, shared in his father's immortality.

The strict friendship and more than brotherly love which subsisted between these chiefs was most remarkable. Whether in peace or war they were always together; they had the same designs, the same pursuits, and were sway'd by the same spirit—insomuch that none could be Pollux's friend without being beloved by Castor; none could be Castor's foe without being also the enemy of Pollux.

These chiefs atchieved together many noble adventures and were the companions of Jason, when he sailed to fetch the golden fleece from Colchis, at which time when the ship Argo was in danger from a storm, two strange fires were seen harmlessly playing round the heads of these youths, after which a calm ensued.---They took the city of Athens and recovered their sister Helena, who had

been

been stolen away by Theseus, being at the same time so merciful that they spared all the citizens.---After this, in a battle which they fought with Lyncæus and Ida the sons of Aphareus, near the mountain Taygetus, Castor (the mortal brother) was slain by Lyncæus, as Lyncæus was by Pollux, who not consoled by revenging his brother's death begged of Jupiter to make him immortal, which request not being granted, he intreated that he might bestow half his own immortality upon his brother, so that they might live and die by turns, to which Jupiter assented; but afterwards both were received into heaven, ranked with the Gods and being placed among the stars, were known by the name of *Gemini*. *

Thus far the fable, which has carried friendship and brotherly love to the greatest height possible---As to the truth of the story, it may seem that these brother chiefs were remarkable for their agreement in every thing, and by their union performed many great exploits------At length, Castor being killed,

and

---

* Or the Twins.

and Pollux having flain Lyncæus, now finding it impoffible to live without his brother, fought the firft occafion of falling in battle, and thus fhared in his death to whom all his wifhes could not reftore life once departed.

THIS is a fit Emblem of brotherly love, and of the advantages arifing from focial connexions---Man was by Nature framed for fociety, and there can be no happinefs below without its benefits---It is by this that we mutually fupply each others wants, and enjoy thofe bleffings of life, which without it we never could purchafe.

Friendfhip is the deareft of all focial ties, and adds the higheft relifh to thefe bleffings. There is not in the world fo unhappy a man as he who has not a friend, while he who is poffefied of fuch a jewel as a true one, may bear up under the ftorms of affliction, and rife fuperior to the frowns of Fortune.

EMBLEM

EMBLEM XII.

Of the Use of Time.

TRUE to the Sun the Dial still abides,
And points Time's course minutely as it glides,
This bids us hasten to be wise and shew,
How rapid in their course the minutes flow,
Seize on the winged hours without delay,
Nor trust to-morrow while we live to day.

Time well employ'd is a most certain gain,
Earnest of pleasure, remedy for pain;
The chief of blessings on its course attends,
Since on its use Eternity depends,

BEHOLD

BEHOLD how true the Dial is to the Sun, and how exactly it marks the hours whose course might otherwise pass unnoticed or unknown.

This useful invention we owe to the mathematicians of ancient days, who thus furnished men with the means of accurately distinguishing the different parts of the day, and dividing them into equal portions, whereby labour and rest, study and amusement were better regulated, and the waste of time seen in a moment, without the trouble of tedious calculations.

The Romans (masters of the world) were at one time so ignorant of the use of Dials that having taken one at the siege of an enemy's city, the consul ordered it without any alteration to be fixed up at Rome; but as it was not calculated for the meridian of that place, it went wrong, a thing which surprized every body till at last a mathematician told them the reason of it and remedied the defect. Dials, and various other methods of marking the hour were used in Rome ever afterwards.

NOTHING can be more useful to us than that which points out the swift flight of time, and shews us how our days draw on to a conclusion, even while we are revelling in the summer and the pride of life.

The Dial is a kind of silent monitor, which, by informing us how the hours fleet away, seems to exhort us to make a proper use of them, and not to waste those precious moments which an hour will come when we shall think of more worth than all the riches of the earth, and which then, all the riches of the earth will not be sufficient to purchase for us.

Every good and wise man will at certain periods examine his own actions, and see what use he has made of past time, and praise or censure himself accordingly. A celebrated poet says

"——Ev'ry Ghost of my departed hours,
" Or smiles an *Angel*, or a *Fury* frowns."

Such

Such an examination will never fail to convince us that we cannot be too careful how we spend the present time; since to employ that well will be the only means of our enjoying that satisfaction here, which will be to us a sort of earnest of our future happiness.

EMBLEM

EMBLEM XIII.

Of Human Grandeur.

BEHOLD how sacred majesty is torn
With racking pains, with care and anguish worn,
While the poor shepherd-boy the time beguiles
With rural sports and unaffected smiles.

'Tis not in grandeur, peace of mind to give,
Nor live those happiest who in splendor live,
Content alone those blessings can bestow,
Which teach the mind with heart-felt joy to glow:
Banish wan care, and all her dismal train,
And give true pleasure, unallay'd by pain.

HAPPINESS is not to be bought with gold, nor secured by the charms of grandeur. Behold here the Queen oppressed with grief flies to solitude and melancholy shades, where she sits overwhelmed with sorrow, and is almost persuaded to put an end to her own existence. —Her state divided by factions, and her private peace of mind destroyed by public cares she remains a melancholy instance of the troubles that attend on greatness, and the sacrifice those make who exchange their tranquility for crowns and sceptres, and their peace for the splendor of dominion.

Not so the Shepherd-Boy; he, though poor, is contented; he rises in health and he lies down in happiness.---The sun is now set; he has folded his flock, and returns home whistling over the plains ;---Majesty beholds his rustic gaiety, and sickens at the sight. She cannot taste those pleasures which dilate his breast, nor share in his rustic joy.---The event is, that she pines to death with sorrow, he lives happy in rural simplicity, and in the enjoyment

joyment of his wishes, because all his wishes are moderate.

FELICITY dwells not with princes;-- she is not the guest of the great ones of the earth. It is long since she fled from palaces, and retired to the scenes of simple nature, to dwell in rural quiet and become the companion of the harmless village swain.

Yet not there alone does she reside: Would you trace her dwelling, you must follow the footsteps of content, and the track will lead you to her peaceful mansion.

But forget not that, as content is never to be found except in the paths of virtue, if you deviate from *her* ways you must never expect to find the road to happiness;---you will become a wanderer, and the hope of your pilgrimage will be lost.

For these three are as inseparable as fire, light, and heat; where the one is, there you will find the others, and the reward shall be such as will far transcend the pains you may be at in acquiring such an inestimable treasure.

In the mean time, envy not the acquisitions of others; for that is base and selfish; neither say within yourself, "Such an one is happy, whilst I am exposed to adversity."

For you know not the secrets of men's hearts; and it may be, that the person whom you esteem happy is a prey to corroding grief, and pines in secret anxiety. At least, know this: That the state of no human being can be determined till death closes the scene;---and the last end of the *good* only can be *happy*. Emulate their virtues, and, doubtless, you shall share in their felicity.

EMBLEM

EMBLEM XIV.

OF WISDOM.

BEHOLD with graceful mien the heavenly maid,
Shines forth in strong and glitt'ring arms array'd!
The power of wisdom in her looks she shews,
And stands the terror of an Host of Foes.

Let PALLAS' arts your ev'ry action guide,
And more in wisdom than in strength confide,
If you with virtue and with prudence arm.
No fraud can reach you, and no strength can harm:
Safe in your self, your foes you may defy,
And vice and folly from your face shall fly.

PALLAS

PALLAS, or MINERVA was said to be the daughter of Jupiter; she sprang out of his head in a full assembly of the Gods. She soon gave evident tokens of her divine descent, by her wisdom, the effects of which were seen both in heaven and earth. She assisted her father Jupiter in his war with the giant Titan.—When she had a dispute with Neptune, God of the sea, which of them should give a city a name, it being agreed that the power who produced the most beneficial thing should have that right. Neptune presented them with a horse, an emblem of strength and courage, but Pallas gave them an olive, an emblem of peace and plenty, on which the dispute was determined in her favour, and she called the city *Athens*.

Thus far the fable, the moral of which is plain; wisdom sprang first from the supreme Being, and by that wisdom he overcomes evil.—By wisdom, peace and plenty flourish in cities and civil societies, and by its means private

private men may be enabled to enjoy domestic happiness.

WHEN the Almighty gave King Solomon his choice of blessings, he asked for Wisdom, and length of days, riches and honour were added to them, because God was pleased with his request, as he had asked only that which was fit and necessary.

The man who is armed with true wisdom has little to fear from the assaults of his enemies; because he finds his resource in *himself*; while he that depends only on the help of *others* is often deserted at his need, and finds his mistake when it is too late to rectify it.

Wisdom is the companion of virtue, as folly is the sister of vice, and it is impossible for a wicked man to be truly wise; for if he were so he would see the foolishness of his evil ways and turn from them.--Wisdom is a safeguard and a tower of defence and he that trusts to her will never have reason to repent his confidence.

Be Virtuous, be Wife, and be Happy; for in the true fenfe of the words they are the fame thing, and from virtue and prudence all the good we can hope for in this world is derived, without them we muft expect nothing but mifery and anxiety.

EMBLEM

EMBLEM XV.
Of Instability.

THIS is the syren, whose enchanting song
Draws the unthinking multitude along,
That feeds with faithless Hopes and luring bait
The poor deluded wretch she means to cheat!
Men call her false, inconstant, cruel, vain,
Yet seek her favours with unweary'd pain.
Th' unhappy bear her frowns, still led away
With expectation of a better day,
Th' ambitious court her smiles; but still the wise
Do her and all her gilded pomp despise.

 Her fairy kingdom, her fantastic good
Avoid, and be more certain hopes pursu'd;
Trust not to fickle Fortune's partial pow'r,
But, timely wise, employ the present hour.---

FORTUNE was among the ancient heathens of all powers reprefented as the moſt partial.---The old Romans worſhipped her as a Deity; but at the fame time it is to be obſerved, that they reprefented her as blind and ſtanding on a wheel. Her blindneſs reprefents her undiſcerning partiality, and the wheel her fickleneſs; juſt emblems of her conduct in the diſtribution of thoſe favours which the wife will always learn to contemn.

That the heathen world, who made deities almoſt of every thing, ſhould aſcribe divine honours to Fortune is not at all wonderful-----but in this more enlightened age, it is moſt ridiculous to make a goddeſs of her; and yet what leſs do they do who leave all to her power, and let the feafons pafs away, day and night fucceed to each other without ever thinking how properly to employ them, trufting all to Fortune and to chance, and forgetting that fuccefs attends on honeſt induſtry, and that poverty is the inſeparable companion of idleneſs.

THERE

THERE is not a juster maxim than "That Fortune is the Deity of Fools;" they only worship her, they only leave every thing in her power, while the wise and good man trusts nothing to her but what he cannot help, bears her smiles with equanimity, and her frowns with fortitude.

Fools, on the other hand, not only worship, but in some sense *make* Fortune, according to the old adage; that is, they trust all to chance, and then complain of those evils whereof themselves are authors.

Those who would be candidates for success in life should never rely on so fickle a patroness; in short, they should consider that there is no such thing as chance, but that every

thing

thing depends on their own induſtry, accompanied by the bleſſing of Providence which generally attends the wiſe and virtuous, and is far more proper to truſt to than ſuch a fickle friend as Fortune, who

"Undiſcerning, ſcatters crowns and chains."

EMBLEM

(61)

EMBLEM XVI.

OF IMPROVEMENT.

LO the industrious BEE employs the hours,
  In sipping fragrance from the various flow'rs:
No plant, no herb, that Nature's hand prepares,
But yields her Honey to reward her cares.

Learn by the BEE from each event to find
Some hint of use or profit to your mind:
Nothing so small but you may draw from thence
Improvement for your virtue or your sense.
Honey like this, life's evils will assuage,
And yield you sweets in your declining age.

THE

THE Bee is a noble pattern of induſtry and prudence. She ſettles upon every plant and flower, and makes the moſt inſignificant, nay even the moſt hurtful of them uſeful to her purpoſe.---Thus ſhe toils all the ſummer, while the days are fair, in order to get a ſtock which ſhe lays by to ſerve for winter, when the herbs and flowers are dead, the trees deprived of their leaves, and the weather bad and unfavourable.

Then the Bees retire to their hive, which is formed like a little ſtate and governed by a queen, who diſpenſes juſtice to her ſubjects. It is ſaid that they bury their dead, puniſh criminals and drive the idle (which are called drones) from their hives.---They keep a regular order whether in war or peace, and as ſoon as their Queen dies, appoint another to ſucceed her and rule their little ſtate, which may ſerve as a pattern for a well-ordered community.

THE Bee is one of the aptest emblems of industry and the art of extracting good out of evil, that can be found in Nature. It is endued with an Instinct that Reason itself needs not be ashamed to copy, and its perseverance is an admirable example for the wisest of us to follow.

As the Bee in the summer provides for itself that which may serve for its support in winter; so should we in the summer of our days take care to lay in a store of profitable virtues and good qualities, which may render us justly admired in age, and enable us to set a good example to posterity.

Like that industrious Insect likewise, we should learn to make every occurrence of life serviceable to us; for nothing is so small or minute but it may be made of use, nothing so bad in nature, but that we may draw from it some profit or instruction, and thus by chusing the good, and avoiding the evil, may purchase to ourselves peace here, and the hopes of a brighter reward hereafter.

EMBLEM

EMBLEM XVII.

OF DECEIT.

WOULD'ST thou, unthinking, to the
　　Beast draw near,
Caught by his plaintive cry and fraudful tear,
Ah! fly in time the dreadful stroke of fate
Nor stay to feel it, and be wise too late.

Deceitful men and all their mazes shun,
Nor by dissembled sorrows be undone,
If much they seem their actions to deplore,
Forgive their crimes, but trust their words no
　　more.

THE Crocodile is reported to weep over its prey, and to send forth a piteous and distressful cry, in order to allure men or beasts to its haunts, that it may seize and devour them. This story is variously told. Some say that it devours whatever it catches, all to the head, and then only weeps that no more is left to satisfy its rapacious appetite. It is most likely, on comparing the different accounts, that this animal makes such a noise as other creatures take for a complaint, though probably it is only a sound as common for it to send forth over its prey as the growling of a cat over a mouse. However that be, Crocodile's Tears are become a Proverb, and a moral of sound prudence may be drawn from the Emblem.

AS

AS it is a man's greatest praise "To be wise as a Serpent, and innocent as a Dove," so he who suffers himself to fall into the snares of designing men will quickly put it out of his own power to be of service to the good and virtuous.

No principle is more noble than that of forgiving injuries, and nothing so wicked or unprofitable as a rancorous revenge. Heaven itself commands us to forgive our enemies; but it is the height of folly for us to trust those who have injured us.

There are a set of people, who, like the Crocodile in the Emblem, will even seem to lament over their former injuries in order to have it in their power to do you fresh ones. Of such persons beware. Do *them* no harm but

but take care not to put it into their power to do *you* any.

If you would pafs through life with any degree of fatisfaction, it is necefsary that you be *good* and *prudent*. Wifdom is the fifter of virtue; join them both in your conduct, and if it fhould happen that you do not *enjoy* all the felicity you might expect, you will at leaft have the comfort to *deferve* it.

EMBLEM

(69)

EMBLEM XVIII.
Of Inordinate Desire.

THE busy insect hov'ring round the light
Pleas'd with the taper's beams which gild the night,
Still round and round in giddy circles flies,
Till caught within the scorching blaze it dies.
Ah! silly thing the source of all thy joy,
A beauteous mischief, shines but to destroy,
Ev'n so the youth who burns with wild desires,
Oft falls the victim of unhallow'd fires.

Avoid the glitt'ring evil, shun the snare
Which Sin and Guile for artless youth prepare:
Lest with the Moth one common fate you prove,
And perish by th' excesses which you love.

THE

THE Moth allured by the brightneſs of the candle, plays round the flame, till at laſt it is conſumed by its heat. A fit emblem this, of thoſe unwary ones who play round the verge of evil, till at length they precipitate themſelves into infamy and ruin.---

The fly, and many other winged inſects have the ſame propenſity to hovering round any luminous body, and frequently die by the heat, which is inſeparable from that brightneſs they ſo much deſire; but none of them all ſo frequently find their fate in the blaze as the Moth, which is almoſt as ſure to periſh by the Candle as to perceive its light.--- The Moth feeds chiefly upon cloth and woollen ſtuffs, and is an animal of ſo delicate a texture that a ſlight touch cruſhes it to pieces; it is therefore the laſt creature in the world to ſuſtain the attacks of ſo terrible an enemy as fire; yet this enemy, in the reſemblance of a friend, courts it to draw near, and afterwards works its inevitable deſtruction.

WHAT

WHAT an unhappy ſtate is theirs who will not take warning by the end of others, nor avoid the miſchiefs which have proved fatal to many.

What numbers have experienced the ſame fate with the inſect in the emblem! and yet what numbers are daily running on, in the ſame manner to their ruin, ſporting with vice and folly, and, as it were, making danger their playfellow;---all theſe cannot, or they will not ſee, *That the end of theſe things is death:* they will go on from one ſtep to another, till at laſt it is too late to recede; then they muſt ſink at once in the gulph of miſery, and only leave freſh examples behind them of what was already well enough known, but always too little regarded.

Shun therefore all temptations if you are wiſe, and be not deceived by appearances Vice, folly, and danger, lurk often under the moſt inviting forms; but try the tree; not by its appearance but by its fruit you ſhall know it.

" Sweeteſt

" Sweetest leaves the rose adorn,
" Yet beneath them lurks the thorn;
" Fair and flow'ry is the brake;
" Yet it hides the speckled snake."

Consider and beware; for he who would avoid sorrow, must be wary in his steps, and he who would shun misfortune must be careful to take wisdom for his companion.

EMBLEM

EMBLEM XIX.
Of Temperance.

WHILE drown'd in luxury yon' feſtal train,
Court this frail world's felicity in vain:
Behold the Cynic from his tub derides
Their idle mirth, and laughing ſhakes his ſides!
He who the world's great maſter* could contemn,
Might ſit, at eaſe and laugh at vice and them,
Few were his wants, and therefore few his woes:
He who has nought to loſe no terrors knows;
Not riches but contentment muſt procure
Our peace below, and make our bliſs ſecure.

Learn nought to covet: prize what is your own,
And you're more bleſt than he who fills a throne.

E   DIO-

---
* Alexander the Great.

DIOGENES was a Grecian Philosopher who much admired poverty, and placed his chief happiness in content. His method of living, however, was extraordinary, for, instead of a house, he dwelt under the covert of a tub, from whence e laughed at the luxuries of the Great, and even went so far as to speak against the use of what are generally deemed the necessaries of life, almost all of which he contrived to subsist without; insomuch that one day, seeing a boy drink out of the hollow of his hand, he broke his pitcher, saying that nothing was necessary to him which it was possible for any one to do without,

When Alexander for his conquests, surnamed the Great, the son of Philip, King of Macedon once made him a visit, and asked him, what he should do for him? "Nothing (replied the Cynic) but stand out of my sunshine, and do not deprive me of that which thou can'st not give me."---In so little estimation did he hold princes or their favours. To say the truth his chief aim being content, and his conduct being founded on the maxim, " That

"That he who has least wants is the happiest man," if his wants were really as few as the supplies he afforded them, he might not unreasonably be supposed to be as happy as any one.

He was a great declaimer against vice in general, and against luxury in particular: and his raillery and that of his sect was so sharp that their countrymen called them Cynics, that is, Snarlers, and this is the appellation by which they are known wherever their names are mentioned in history.

———

THERE can be no doubt but that the happiness of every man must in a great measure depend on the disposition of his mind; else should we not every day see some people happy with every thing that, to all outward appearance, could contribute to their felicity, whilst others, scarcely possessed of necessaries, seem merry and happy.

This was in some degree the case of that philosopher who, passing through a public fair,

fair, exclaimed "How many things are here which I do not want?"

In short as a late celebrated poet observes
He laugh'd at all the vulgar's cares and
    fears,
At their vain triumphs, and their vainer
    fears:
An equal temper in his mind he found,
When fortune flatter'd him, or when she
    frown'd.

EMBLEM

EMBLEM XX.

Of false Friendship.

THE Stag once wounded, 'tis in vain he flies,
In vain to mingle with the herd he tries;
The herd avoid him, as mark'd out for death,
Till in despair he draws his latest breath,
His wayward fate all friendly aid denies:
Deserted at his utmost need, he dies.

So those false friends whom worldly int'rests sway
When mischiefs threaten will fly far away,
Bask in thy sunshine; but in evil times
And louring days, seek out for warmer climes.
Chuse then with caution, if thou wouldst succeed;
A friend in poverty's a friend indeed.

IT has often been remarked of the stag, that, being wounded by the hunters, he attempts to take shelter among the first herd of deer that he espies, while these, on their part, as industriously avoid him, and to keep off danger from themselves, like false friends, desert him, and abandon him to his fate, which after many endeavours to escape, he generally meets with a courage inspired by despair, and dies fighting with his enemies.— The desertion of his species is beautifully pictured by Shakespear in his play called As you Like it, in the following lines:

—————————" A poor sequester'd Stag
" 'That from the hunter's aim had ta'en a hurt,
" Did come to languish there;
" The wretched animal heav'd forth such groans
" That their discharge did stretch his leathern coat,
" Almost to bursting, and the big round tears
" Cours'd one another down his innocent nose

" In

" In piteous chace;——Anon a carelefs
    herd
" Full of the pafture jumped along by
    him,
" And never ftay'd to greet him---Aye!
    quoth Jacques,
" Sweep on, you fat and greafy citizens
" Tis juft the fashion"---

This creature if he efcapes the hunters generally lives to a great age---Some authors fay he attains to 300 years, but this feems to be a fable: However, that he is a very long-lived animal is clear from many circumftances inconteftably authenticated: Nature has endued him with a remarkable fwiftnefs of foot, and the branches which vegetate from his head are equally ufeful and ornamental.

THERE cannot be a fitter emblem of falfe friendfhip than that which is here exhibited---The Stag is wounded; He flies from his purfuers, who have marked him out for death, he feeks, by mingling with the crowd, to efcape their notice. Where fhould he hope for fhelter but among his own kind,---perhaps the

the very herd of which he was once the leader? He throws himself therefore upon their protection: How vain are his designs!---They are resolved not to share in his misfortunes. They fly, and teach him too late how little he has to hope from their kindness---He falls ---and the consequence is that among all these, every one in his turn experiences the same treatment from his fellow.

Just so it fares with those friendships which are founded only upon interest, which have neither piety, virtue, nor mutual benevolence for their basis---In prosperity, these men will be ever ready at your command, either because you do not want them, or because they know you will overpay their services. Change the scene to adversity, and they change with it---They desert you---you will find no shelter with them, but, like the deer in the fable, each will shift for himself and leave you to your fate.

Be careful then how you chuse a friend, which is the greatest of all earthly acquisitions; and above all things remember, that can be no real friendship which is founded merely upon interest.

EMBLEM

EMBLEM XXI.

Of Education.

SEE in what evil plight yon' Vine appears,
Nor spreading leaves, nor purple clusters bears;
But if around the elm her arms she throw,
Or by some friendly prop supported grows,
Soon shall the stem be clad with foliage green,
And cluster'd grapes beneath the leaves be seen.

Thus prudent care must rear the youthful mind
By love supported, and with toil refin'd:
'Tis thus alone the human plant can rise,
Unpropp'd, it droops, and unsupported, dies.

THE Vine never flourishes without a prop or support. Like the fruit it bears, it is of a social nature, and rewards the friendly shade which supports it with its purple treasures. But if it is suffered to creep along without a prop, it will most certainly disappoint the hopes of the planter, and prove barren and useless.

THIS is a fit Emblem of Youth, which if left to itself will never grow up in wisdom or in virtue.------To education alone must children be indebted for their morals, and the care of the parents is always visible in the conduct of their offspring.

When a youth has received a virtuous and liberal education, no gratitude can be sufficient to discharge the debt he owes to his parents; since he is not only obliged to them for his Being, but also for all his hopes of peace here, and of eternal happiness hereafter.

On the other hand, he who has been neglected in his youth has a heavy accusation to bring

bring against those who reared him, when he comes to years of maturity! Evil inclinations, if not checked, will grow amazingly upon us, while good ones, if they be not properly encouraged, will fade and die away; and that will be too late deplored in age which might have been remedied in our earlier years.

How careful then ought parents and guardians to be of their charge, of which they must one day render up an account, where no idle excuses will be admitted, no evasion, nor equivocation can avail them!

If it be then found that they have been careless in this great work, how poignant will be their shame, and how severe their punishment!

But if they have faithfully discharged this trust committed to them by Heaven itself, how great will be their honour, how glorious the crown of their reward!

The education of children is indeed a matter of such consequence that it concerns not only private persons but the public in general

and

and that nation will always be the moſt virtuous, and the moſt reſpectable, whoſe youth are educated with the greateſt care, and are earlieſt inſtructed in the duties of men and of chriſtians.

Theſe, like the generous Vine, will fully repay the pious care of the planter, and, while they are known by their fruit, will reflect honour upon the hands that reared them.

EMBLEM

EMBLEM XXII.

OF RESISTING THE EVIL PRINCIPLE.

BY great Apollo's arms the Python slain,
Lies stretch'd o'er many an acre on the plain;
The world rejoices from the monster freed,
The Godhead triumphs in the glorious deed.
For feats like these, heroic chiefs of old,
In Fame's bright temple highest honour hold.

With valiant heart proceed in virtue's ways,
And gain the tribute of immortal praise;
The monster Vice with all your pow'rs engage,
And rise the Phœbus of another age.

THE Serpent Python was a monster, which according to the fabulous account sprung from the mud and stagnated waters that the general deluge left behind it.

This monster, the God Apollo, (who is also called Phœbus, engaged) and destroyed it with his unering arrows! for which service divine honours were paid him, and the Pythian games established. He had a celebrated temple at Delphos, where oracles were delivered in his name by a priestess called Pythia, and was next to Jupiter the most esteemed of all the heathen Gods.

The fable signifies that the deluge left behind it certain flagnant waters, and these produced pestilential vapours, which, however, at length the beams of Apollo, Phœbus, or the Sun, exhaled, and destroyed their noxious quality.

The moral is, that vice and oppression ought to be courageously resisted, and that those who do good to their fellow creatures deserve to receive public honours at their hands.

———————

IF we mean to atchieve praise-worthy actions, we must not be daunted at difficulties, nor terrified by opposition We must resolve to vanquish these obstacles which may arise, and this resolution will be half the victory.

We must moreover be ever ready prepared, at every occasion to resist the Evil Principle, which like the Python, in the Emblem, lays all waste before him. Clad in the armour of virtue, we must advance boldly to the combat; we must conquer all bad inclinations, and with the assistance of the Divine Grace, make war upon the depravity and wickedness of our own nature. This is the conquest we

shall

shall find hardest to gain, but when obtained it will fully recompence our toils; since he that has his paffions at command is greater than he who rules a kingdom, and the man that vanquishes himself is greater than he who triumphs over an enemy.

EMBLEM

EMBLEM XXIII.

Of Fortitude.

SAFE in its strength, the Rock's broad base derides,
The roaring tempests and the raging tides,
Unmov'd tho' Boreas bluster from on high,
Or Ocean lift his billows to the sky:
Its fix'd foundations which by Heav'n were cast
When Time began, with Time itself shall last.

Be strong, be stedfast, in fair virtue's cause,
Nor fear reproof, nor covet vain applause;
Heed not of evil tongues the envious strife,
Nor the loud storms that rage through human life:
On truth's firm basis let your hopes remain,
And seas may rage, and tempests roar in vain.

A ROCK

A ROCK in the midst of a troubled ocean, attacked by tempests, and beaten by the boiling surges, is a just resemblance of a virtuous man bearing up under the storms of affliction, and resisting every temptation to abandon his innocence. This is he who has built his house on a Rock: the rains and the winds may come, and beat upon it, but in vain; because its foundation is stedfast and cannot be removed. But he whose constancy is not proof against the storms of adversity is indeed like one who has founded his house on the sand, which the first tempest will be likely to overthrow, and to sweep away its remembrance from under heaven.--To such a man what avails it that he has been accounted virtuous, if he falls off in the day of trial, if at length, when he is weighed in the ballance he is found wanting?---His good deeds will be forgotten, but his offence, will be had in perpetual remembrance.

ADVERSITY is the test of constancy, it is the fiery trial which when the virtuous have
gone

gone through, they are found as pure gold, neither diminished in weight nor value---

It is an easy thing for a man to possess himself in the summer and sunshine of life; it is easy for him to boast that virtue which never yet was tried, and to boast of that fortitude which he has never yet had occasion to exert; but true magnanimity and greatness of soul are found in supporting evils with resignation, and resisting temptations with resolution.

It is by the test of misfortune that the greatest and best of men have been proved; it is to their noble behaviour under it that they owe the titles of Good and Great.---The saints and martyrs among the primitive christians, and Socrates, among the heathens, dying fearless and undaunted for the testimony of truth, are characters which will ever be justly admired in this world as doubtless they were rewarded in a better state.

Learn then to copy such great examples, and hold fast the truth even to death; this is to lay your foundation on a Rock, which defies the tempest and stands secure amidst the roaring waves of the ocean, which endeavour in vain to shake it, because its basis is stedfast and immoveable.

EMBLEM

(93)

EMBLEM XXIV.

Of the Use of Self-Denial.

WITH hasty steps, at the first dawn of day,
The chearful traveller pursues his way;
But tired at noon he seeks a shady grove,
Of lofty trees, whose branches meet above:
Conceal'd beneath the grass the Serpent lies,
The swain draws near and by his venom dies.

Thus he who, leaving virtue's sacred ways,
Securely through the paths of pleasure strays,
Wounded by vice, his peace and honour lost,
Buys late experience at too dear a cost:
To him who *perseveres* alone are giv'n,
Fair fame on earth and endless bliss in Heav'n.

A SERPENT concealed in the grass is an apt emblem of fraud and vice, concealed under specious appearances.---The Traveller goes on his road with chearfulness, during the morning hours: he doubts not but he shall soon get to his journey's end, and expects not to meet with the least obstacle in his way.

But when he feels the heat increasing, his vigour begins to relax. When the hours of noon arrive, he is absolutely weak and faint. He beholds a wood spread its inviting shade; he considers not that to enter it, is to deviate from his road; he thinks not what danger he may encounter there. All his attention is taken up in relieving himself from a present inconvenience.

He enters the grove, he loses himself among its cool and agreeable windings. When he would return, he finds himself perplexed as in a maze, and before he can regain the road is bitten by a venomous reptile which was concealed from his sight among the grass. ---He now wishes he had borne the heat of
the

the day: His blood is consumed with fires far more intolerable. He falters, he sinks under his pains, and falls a victim to his own imprudence.

———

VIRTUE is never safe but when she is secured by the guard of prudence: Discretion is her handmaid and Wisdom her counsellor and instructor.

Caution is a necessary lesson to be learned by youth, and perseverance one of the best qualities they can be endowed with.

When Fortune smiles upon us, it is easy to go on in the practice of virtue; and a man may easily obtain the reputation of being *good* when he is so circumstanced that he must become a monster of vice to be *wicked*.

But this is counting his advantage before the field is won. Let him be subject to the rough storms of adversity. Let him bear the heat and burden of the day.

Will he not *then* turn aside to the paths of pleasure, and seek for relief in the bowers of dissipation?

It is thus that many are lost who have begun a good work, but have not had courage and resolution to go through with it. They have turned aside from virtue; all their good works are forgotten, they have lost their reward, and their memory is a bye-word to posterity.

But you who would attain to the end of your labours, follow not after their example. Be you virtuous, and to your *virtue* join *prudence*, be prudent also, and to your prudence join *perseverance*; so shall you not fall into the snares of pleasure; nor feel the envenomed stings of guilt and of remorse, whose bill is sharper than that of the serpent, and whose poison is more deadly than that of the venomous adder.

EMBLEM

EMBLEM XXV.

Of the Danger of Temptation.

THE silly Fish, while playing in the brook,
Hath gorg'd and swallow'd the destructive hook;
In vain he flounces on the quiv'ring hair,
Drawn panting forth to breathe the upper air.
Caught by his folly—in the glitt'ring bait,
He meets his ruin, and submits to fate.

Avoid base bribes; the tempting lure displayed,
If once you seize you perish self-betray'd.
Be slow to take, when strangers haste to give,
Lest of your ruin you the price receive.

THE simple Fish sports on the surface of the clear streams, while the wily Angler plies his rod and line;---often the timid animal approaches the bait, and as often he retires from it, till at last, just as the sun shrouds his radiance behind a cloud, he ventures to jump at the fictitious fly, swallows it at once and with it swallows the bearded hook. That moment seals his ruin; smarting from the wound, he struggles, and endeavours to free himself, but in vain. The Angler, giving full play to the line, permits him to run away with it. But this struggle only tends to make his ruin more certain. He is soon tired out, and then being lifted out of the water proves an easy prey to his foe. He pants, he expires in agonies, yet owes his destruction to a slender hair : so often do seeming trifles tend to ruin and perdition.

———————

WHAT a fit Emblem is this of those heedless persons who suffer themselves to be eluded by glittering temptations, or drawn into

into snares by the artifices of the vicious and designing.

If for a while, like the fish, they play about the hook, yet in some unguarded moment, when the light of their reason is obscured, they seize the specious bait, and then they find all their struggles ineffectual. He who has had the art to catch, has generally the judgement to secure his prey. Such an one will but smile at their vain attempts to recover their liberty, while he is sensible these only serve still farther to enthral them. The dye is cast, and they become the victims of their own imprudence.

The offers of some men are dangerous: be not therefore led away by specious appearances: think before you act, and let the character of the giver and the conditions he is likely to exact be well considered before you receive the gift. If it be the price of vice or folly, shun it, as you hope for peace and honest fame: Each temptation you have avoided, will by reflexion strengthen you against the next:

custom

custom will make the most difficult self-denials easy, and by one victory you will be enabled to gain another. You will be thus delivered from the snares of vice, and folly shall not triumph over your fall.

EMBLEM

EMBLEM XXVI.
Of Perseverance.

JASON, a bold advent'rer, fail'd to claim
   The precious prize which rais'd his country's fame—
His veffel bore the flow'r of ancient Greece,
To Colchis' fhore to claim the golden fleece:
But firft the brazen footed bulls he train'd
And with hard yokes their ftubborn necks reftrain'd;
Sow'd ferpent's teeth from which immediate rofe,
A grove of lances and a hoft of foes;—
And charm'd the watchful dragon to repofe.
Thefe toils o'erpaft in peace he ends his days,
And gains the tribute of immortal praife.

  Be refolute in good, and you will find
All evils fhrink before a conftant mind.

THE golden fleece was the skin of a golden ram which had been offered up to Jupiter, and was kept at Colchis, but on the condition of being surrendered to any man who could tame the King's brazen-footed bulls which belched out fire and smoke, gain the victory over an armed troop that were to rise out of serpent's teeth sown in the earth, and charm to sleep a wakeful dragon which guarded the splendid prize.

To atchieve this adventure several Grecian heroes sailed for Colchis, the chief of whom was Jason the son of Æson, a chief renown'd for courage and fortitude, who by the assistance of certain charms which he received from Medea, the Colchian monarch's daughter, yoked the bulls, overcame the armed men by a stratagem, caused the dragon to fall into a deep sleep and brought away the golden fleece, together with the princess who helped him to obtain it.

The vessel they sailed in was named Argo, from whence these adventurers were termed Argo-

Argonauts: This was said to be the first expedition of any consequence that the Greeks ever undertook, and those who were concerned in it were some of the most famous heroes in fabulous history.

This is the tenor of the story, which is greatly mixed with fable. The truth seems to be, that Jason and his companions failed to establish a gainful commerce at Colchis. in this their expedition they met with many obstacles from the savage manners of the people they had to deal with, but at last by perseverance overcame them, and happily returned to their native country, crowned with all the success their warmest wishes could have induced them to expect.

———————

EXAMPLES like these of fortitude and perseverance in all laudable undertakings for the benefit of ourselves, our friends, or our country, carry their application with them, which can never be too much inculcated or attended to.

If, like Jason, we would bear away the prize, like him we must learn to deserve it; we must hazard ourselves against the fierce, we must not be afraid to oppose the strong, when virtue and the duty we owe to Heaven and to our country demand it. Above all things, we must learn to curb our immoderate passions; these are the fiery bulls which we must break to the yoke. We must conquer the host of temptations, and charm to sleep the Evil Principle which is always ready to molest us.

Finally we must never hope to vanquish the stubborn temper of others, till we have first learned to subdue our own, nor must we ever expect to atchieve any great actions unless we are endowed with an unconquerable firmness and perseverance.

EMBLEM

EMBLEM XXVII.

Of Vain Pursuits.

FROM sultry noon till night's dull
    shades descend,
Behold the boy his fruitless chace attend,
To gain the insect's painted wings he flies
And pleas'd at last obtains the gaudy prize;
But whilst its beauties he surveys with joy,
Those hands which seize them fatally destroy.

Ev'n so those pleasures which we sigh to
    gain,
And sacrifice our quiet to obtain,
With gaudy flutt'rings, tempt us to pursue,
But while we grasp them, vanish from our
    view,
Or, gain'd, but ill reward our labour past,
Crush'd, as we seize them, by our eager haste.

THE simple Boy, smitten with the gaudy colours of the Butterfly, chaces it from flower to flower with the utmost eagerness.—The fluttering insect still flies before him, still eludes his pursuit. At one time when he thinks he has it just within his grasp, it slips away, and soars aloft in air; at another, it skulks behind the leaves of a plant, and hides itself from his curious search.

The hours slip away unperceived, and the wanton loses himself while he is pursuing his prey.—The chace began at noon; he sustains the heat of the meridian hours; the day declines, and he is not yet at the end of his labour.

But, at length just at the time of the sun's setting, he surprizes the gay fluttering insect, in the cup of a blue bell. Eagerly he hastes to catch it, he squeezes the sides of the flower together to prevent the escape of his captive; he does indeed most effectually prevent it, but at the same time he defeats his own end, for he crushes the insect to pieces; and thus by his own eagerness loses the fruit of his toil, and destroys that beauty which he coveted to possess.

THIS is an apt Emblem of the impetuosity of youth, which with a blind precipitancy pursues vain pleasures that never can afford any solid enjoyment.

Passion is ever fierce, headlong, and regardless of consequences; it is ready to encounter all opposition, to run through every danger, for the most trifling acquisition, and its hurry often destroys the objects on which its wishes have been set, by no other means than its eagerness to possess them.

Passion thus indulged can never contribute any thing to felicity; and he who knows not what it is to be moderate in the pursuit of pleasures will never know what it is truly to enjoy them.

And

And moreover, we should ever
"Avoid to take the life we cannot give,
"Since all things have an equal right to live."

EMBLEM

EMBLEM XXVIII.
OF AMBITION.

WHY would yon' Eagle proudly foar
 so high,
And ftrive to emulate the diftant fky,
What? Sees fhe not the weight, and ftrait'ning
 band,
That all her pow'r with double force with-
 ftand.
In vain, fond bird, your pinions you extend,
Check'd in your flight, to earth you muft de-
 fcend,
Ev'n fo would mad ambition wildly tow'r,
Boundlefs his wifh, but limited his pow'r.

Remember all things have a certain bound,
Which once attain'd your *ne plus ultra's*
 found:
Ambition fhun, if you would tafte of peace,
For while its views extend, its forrows ftill
 increafe.

THE

THE Eagle is generally esteemed the chief of birds—It flies higher than all others, and builds its nest in the tops of the loftiest trees, or on high rocks, poising it with stones in the former case to prevent its falling. The long life and sharp sight of this bird have been much exaggerated: It has been reported to live more than a century, and to fly always directly against the sun fixing its eyes on him in his greatest splendor.----Thus much however, is certain, that the Eagle possesses a very piercing sight, and lives to a great age. It is a bird of prey, like the Vulture, and others of that kind, and will, sometimes, even attack living quadrupeds.

The Eagle has ever been reckoned an emblem of ambition. It was esteemed sacred to Jupiter among the heathens, as being set apart to carry his thunder, and was always represented as one of the symbols of that god.

———————

IN the Emblem before us, we have an apt representation of ambition, which in spite of
all

all its towering, must still be confined to limits, a circumstance perfectly against its nature, and which never fails of administering cause of anxiety to its possessor.

Can there be more striking instances of this truth than those which are exhibited to us in the person of Alexander, surnamed the *Great*, son of Philip, King of Macedon.--- This prince was contented to renounce his father, and travel over burning desarts, to get himself acknowledged the son of the god Jupiter.---The same prince having conquered Persia, and India and most of those parts known to the Greeks, wept because he supposed there was no more to conquer. Ridiculous madness! Insatiable ambition! This son of the great Jove died of a surfeit at Babylon in the bloom of his years, and being too proud to admit that any one deserved to succeed him, he left his empire to be divided and torn with intestine broils, which in a course of years made it an easy prey to the Romans, who led the last King of Macedonia in triumph through the streets of Rome, and, at length, starved him to death in a dungeon.

Such

Such are the fruits of ambition. It was the firſt, and continues to be one of the greateſt of follies---for, "by that ſin fell the Angels; how can man then (the image of his maker) hope to win by it?"

EMBLEM

EMBLEM XXIX.

OF THE REWARD OF VICE.

LO, here the nymph, by her own father's doom,
Condemn'd alive to perish in her tomb,
Because she yielded to a flatt'ring tale,
And o'er her virtue let her love prevail;
Her groans no pity from a parent claim,
She sinks bereft, at once, of life and fame.

Those who quit virtue Heav'n itself forsakes,
And of their suff'rings no compassion takes;
Whom Heav'n forsakes must seek relief in vain,
From their own parents and their kindred train:
Shunn'd like a thing accurs'd in dust they fall
The dread of many, and the scorn of all.

LEUCOTHOE, was the daughter of Orchamus, King of Perſia, With her the god Apollo is ſaid to have been in love. She was not virtuous or prudent enough to reſiſt his ſolicitations, and they carried on a correſpondence together which they thought to be a private one; but this being diſcovered by one of Apollo's old favourites, the King her father was ſoon made acquainted with it. Being a haughty prince, he could not endure the diſgrace which was put on his family by this accident, and therefore, notwithſtanding all his daughter's prayers and tears, commanded her to be buried alive. This terrible ſentence was accordingly executed, without her receiving any relief from her lover. However after her death the fable ſays, Apollo whoſe aid was too late to ſave her, cauſed the frankincenſe tree which weeps perpetually, to ſpring out of her grave.

THERE is a fine contraſt between Daphne's ſtory and this of Leucothöe. The former eluded the ſnares of vice and perſevering in defence of her honour was beloved and honoured

honoured in her end: The latter yields to unlawful solicitations, and perishes miserably, neglected and despised by all, at the express command of her father, and without having received the aid she might have expected from her lover, who appears, but too late to save her, and only pays a sort of mournful tribute to her memory.

If we desire to be had in estimation by others, or assisted by them in time of distress, we must first learn what is due to ourselves and act up to the dignity of our own Nature, by not being defiled with vice, and so rendering ourselves unworthy of support and assistance.

Neither are we to expect that those who delude us into evil actions, will be always ready to protect us in the commission of them.---The greater they are, the farther will they be removed from us in the day of necessity; and if they have any power, they will use it to screen themselves.---A fruitless pity is the most that can be expected from them, and that only expressed when it is too late for their compassion to reflect any dishonour on themselves or to give us any consolation.

Finally,

Finally, if we expect or desire that Heaven should not forsake us, we should not forsake Heaven, and if we shudder at the punishment of an offender we should learn betimes to avoid the crimes which occasioned it.

EMBLEM

EMBLEM XXX.

OF THE JUST PUNISHMENT OF THE SELFISH.

THE grov'ling beast whose savage strength destroys,
The flow'ry garden that the swain enjoys;
Shews that when in his beastly pastime slain,
His death alone can be his master's gain.---

The wicked selfish man who gripes the poor,
And rates the injur'd orphan from his door;
Like the base Swine his neighbour's peace destroys,
And all his pow'r in evil still employs;
When all his riches he has left behind,
Dying, alone he benefits mankind.

THE Hog is of all beasts the most savage and untractable; it is swayed by nothing but a savage fierceness and a stupid gluttony. Of most other creatures made for the use of man, some profit may be gained in their life. This in its death alone is useful, and then it is more profitable than any animal of its own dimensions.

When Boars run wild in the woods they are the most dreadful of all beasts, first because of their great fierceness, and secondly on account of their stupidity, which is so great that it makes them disregard their safety, and rush on their own certain destruction in order to accomplish that of those whom they engage with.--In short it is become such a proverb, by which to express obstinacy, gluttony and many evil qualities that to be said to resemble a Swine is the worst comparison a man can be subject to.

NATURE seems to have set us examples of good and evil qualities, even among the brute creation, Thus the Lamb for Innocence, the Horse for Courage, the Ox for Patience, the Serpent for Deceit, and the Swine in the Emblem before us, for Fierceness and Sensuality.

It is a melancholy consideration that some men seem to have taken pattern by this groveling beast, that they lead a life of gluttony and drunkenness, are entirely wrapped up in self-love and lost to every thought of charity and good-will to their neighbours.

Such men can indeed do no other good to the world but by their deaths, when if they have any riches they may perhaps leave them to others who will make a better use of those gifts than they have done.

There-

Therefore, if you would have men wish you life and prosperity, live in such a manner as to be serviceable to society; for depend on it if you copy the Swine's manners, you will share the same fate, that none will be sorry for your misfortune, or your death, while they can reap nothing but injury from your life and prosperity.

EMBLEM

EMBLEM XXXI.

OF PRECIPITATION.

WHAT means that rash and heedless
    charioteer,
Down the steep rock to urge his mad career?
Sees he not round him various dangers grow,
High cliffs above and yawning deeps below?
Yet down the dreary, dreadful path he hies,
Madly meets ruin, and despairing dies.

So some wild youth to passion gives the
    rein,
And buys short pleasure with an age of pain,
For him destruction spreads the fatal snare,
He sinks in gulphs of mis'ry and despair.

THIS Emblem has formerly been used by Plato the Greek philosopher. He used to say that the soul or reason of man represented a Charioteer, and his passions wild horses, which it was his business to restrain, lest they should hurry him on to ruin and destruction.

Certainly it is but a sad consideration that some men should not have so much government over themselves, as by habit they acquire over their beasts---These are seen generally to turn, to stand still, to proceed this way or that, or to stop in the midst of their career as the driver would have them, and if he be a skilful man it is seldom that we have an instance of his failing in governing them.

But how many instances have we of men's passions not submitting to the government of their reason? a sad example of people's neglecting great matters, to attend to small ones,
and

and thinking it less worth their while to mind the management of themselves than that of their horses.

———————

IF you would ever wish to enjoy peace here or hereafter, you must learn that great and useful lesson, to controul your passions;--- like *fire* and *water* they are good servants but terrible masters, and if you do not learn early to command them, they will certainly command you, and, in the end, will lead you to inevitable destruction.

Defer not this till to-morrow; to-morrow may never come, or, coming, it may be too late. But above all, if you examine which is the ruling passion, or inclination in your heart, keep a check upon that, and by such a method you will be most likely to bring all the rest under subjection. It is the master-key to every one's breast; it will therefore let you into the secrets of your own heart, and teach you some part of that most useful lesson, the knowledge of yourself, which is preferable to all other sciences in the world. Above all remember that constancy is the bond of piety and self-denial the very test of religion and virtue.

EMBLEM

EMBLEM XXXII.

Of the Changes of Human Affairs

THE beauteous moon renews her faded light,
Not with her own, but borrow'd luftre bright,
Uncertain planet! whofe great changes fhew,
Th' unftable ftate of all things here below,
Tho' now but half her radiant form fhe fhews,
Her waxing luftre every moment grows;
Till to the Sun her glowing face fhe turns,
Drinks all his beams, and in full glory burns.

Thus all things change with time's revolving round,
And nothing permanent on earth is found,
Tho' now but half thy wifhes thou canft fhare,
Succeeding times thy fortune may repair.
But whate'er chance on thy concerns await
Scorn to do ill, in order to be great;
The meed of virtue is as fix'd as Fate.

THE Moon, though a beautiful and an useful planet, yet receives all her light from the Sun, and is but as a mirrour or looking-glafs to reflect his beams——Yet fhe gives us light in his abfence, rules the ebbing and flowing of the tides, and is particularly attended to by phyficians in the treatment of their patients.

Her periods of change in the month are divided into four. The *firft quarter* when fhe fhews but half her face, in the increafe. The *full* when fhe is entirely enlightened.---The *laft quarter* when only half her face is again to be feen, in the decreafe --And the *New Moon* commences immediately after her being entirely darkened.——All thefe are occafioned by her pofition with regard to the Sun; the more of his beams fhe receives, the more light fhe is in a condition of giving, and it is confequently when fhe turns her whole face exactly oppofite to him that fhe is faid to be at the Full, and reflects the ftrongeft luftre.

In the Emblem she appears as just before she enters the first quarter, at which time though she does not impart half the light of the full moon, yet she gives signs of her increase, from whence we may conclude that we shall soon see her in her greatest glory.

THE Moon has ever been reckoned a symbol of inconstancy, from her perpetual changes; yet these are such as God and Nature have appointed for her, and her various course is doubtless as necessary for the universe as the constancy of the most steady fixed star we can observe, or any other principle in Nature.

Why then may we not conclude the same of Fate, whose partiality we are so ready to accuse, when it does not favour us---But who was ever heard to accuse Fate for the good dealt to him, though for aught he knew many worthy people might be the worse for it?

To return to the moral of our Emblem.--- On this very change in the world may we found a syftem of rational philofophy, fince it teaches thofe who poffefs much, not to be too proud of what they may foon be deprived of, and comforts thofe who have but little, and the captive and oppreffed with the thought that a day may come, even in this world, when thefe their forrows fhall have an end; and if not fo, that yet moft certainly time muft by its revolutions bring them eafe, and change their condition and their life together.

Defpond not therefore, though thou art not arrived to the poffeffion of thy wifhes---Think on thefe morals and be wife---Above all things, ftick to virtue for that will be found unchangeable, and will certainly carry its reward with it either here or hereafter.

EMBLEM XXXIII.

OF THE SNARES OF VICE.

AH! see you yonder bird, devoid of care,
Which sang, and flutter'd near the fowler's snare!
Too soon alas! her state she will deplore,
Doom'd to a lonesome cage; to mount no more:
But plaintive notes, imprison'd still to try,
And wish in vain for native liberty.

Beware of vice, whose empire will controll,
The native freedom of a gen'rous soul;
Avoid her snares, where certain mischiefs wait
Nor rush unthinking on destructive fate.

BEHOLD how the silly bird struggles in the snare that the artful fowler has contrived for its destruction.---Too late the poor flutterer finds its fatal error, too late repents its rashness, when confined in a wiry prison, and obliged to pour its complaints in solitude; fit Emblem of a man who by his vices or his follies has forfeited that chief of all blessings heaven-born liberty.

A celebrated English traveller in France mentions a very peculiar story of a bird in a cage, (which just at the time when he was reflecting on the Nature of confinement) suddenly cried " I can't get out"---And this so struck him that it at once convinced him of the blessing of liberty, which he was now disposed to give to the poor bird also, which

still

still continued its note, and as the gentleman was complaining that he could not open the cage, the Starling still cried "No, I can't get out," and still more confirm'd the traveller in his love of native freedom.

LIBERTY is indeed one of the most valuable blessings in the world, and life itself is of little worth without it. For this, wise men have argued, heroes have died, and left the glorious prize to posterity.

Yet after all, it is in vain for any one to suppose himself free who is not also virtuous, when once we give way to our passions like the bird in the emblem, we are caught in the fatal snare which must entangle us, and deprive us of our real liberty.

The

The slaves of vice and passion can never be deemed free, and a slave he ever will be who suffers his own bad inclinations to get the better of him.

EMBLEM

(133)

EMBLEM XXXIV.

Of Passion.

BEHOLD the furious beaſt, more
    fierce he grows!
When the clear ſtream his proper image
    ſhews!
Nor for his own the hideous figure knows.

So could we ſee how paſſion's dreadful
    ſtorm,
And maddiug fury all our ſouls deform,
Eraſe God's image planted in our breaſt,
And change the man into a ſavage beaſt:
We ſhould abhor ourſelves, the ſhape diſown,
And hate the fiend that put our likeneſs on.

THE

THE Lion, the Bull, and other fierce creatures are particularly enraged at viewing their own shape in water or a glass; it is a circumstance which doubles their fury, since they there behold a distorted figure, which instinct impels them to make war upon.

To these animals it is not given to know that the shape they are so much offended with is their own: they are not sensible that their own rage makes them such frightful figures: they take the hateful image for another fierce creature, and immediately commence a fight with it.

Heaven not having bestowed on the Lion and the Bull the sacred gift of reason, their mistake is natural, as their fury is excusable. In both these points they act just as they were ordained to act, and fill up that necessary part of the creation, which for wise ends they were created to occupy: Man alone is blameable when he runs counter to reason, and reduces himself to the situation of the savage animal, whose fury and evil qualities he is absurd enough to imitate.

THERE is not a fiercer fiend than Anger when indulged, nor a passion so detestable in the sight both of God and Man--It leads to all manner of evil; its way is in wickedness, and to those who encourage it, its end must be certain destruction.

The distinction of father, mother, brother, sister, friend, and every tender tie of humanity are lost when it rages, and it tempts men to commit in a moment such enormities as an age of repentance is not sufficient to atone for.

It is a short madness, whose effects are equally terrible in those who indulge it, as in those who are the objects of its rage; it has often led to real madness, to ruin, and to death; and he who gives way to it can no more answer for his actions than if he were drunk or lunatic, or possessed with an evil spirit at the time he is angry and enraged.

In fine, Anger is a vice of such a cast that it debases God's image which is stamped upon our nature, making us rather resemble dæmons than human creatures, and if passionate men

men could have a full and just view of themselves in all their deformity both of soul and body, they must hate themselves, and like the lion in the emblem make war with their own image than which nothing in Nature can be more hideous and detestable.

EMBLEM

(137)

EMBLEM XXXV.
Of Chastity.

DAPHNE, the fairest of the woodland train,
Apollo long had woo'd, but woo'd in vain,
At lengh the god surpriz'd her in the shade,
And strove to gain with promis'd gifts the maid;
Her, still resisting, o'er the plains he chac'd,
But when he thought the nymph to have embrac'd,
Instead of Daphne, bright in blooming charms,
Surpriz'd, he clasped a laurel in his arms.
The tree belov'd still bears his honor'd name,
Emblem of conquest and of deathless fame.

Avoid temptation, though the gilded bait
Be deck'd with all the pomp of guilty state,
Nor with the tempter strive to try your might :—
Retire betimes ;—your conquest is in flight.

DAPHNE

DAPHNE (the daughter of Pencius the river-god) was so beautiful that Apollo or Phœbus, the God of day * was smitten with her, and made her many offers if she would consent to his suit, which she still resisting, he strove at last to accomplish by force that which was denied to his request. But Daphne, finding his purpose, sought her security in flight. Apollo followed with a swiftness not to be matched by mortals, and was just upon the point of overtaking her; when, in the midst of her distress she prayed most earnestly that she might be enabled to preserve her chastity.----Her prayer was heard, and at the instant her pursuer came up with her, he found her changed into a laurel.

Apollo, though disappointed of his purpose could not but admire her constancy; he therefore pronounced the tree his own, and consecrated it as sacred to the reward of virtuous actions.---The laurel has ever since been esteemed as an emblem of excellency either in arms or arts, to those who were crowned

---

* See Pantheon.

crowned with it: And what was once Apollo's love has always been considered as his tree.---So far the ancient fable.

———————

THE application is plain and ſtriking. Nothing ought to be held ſo dear as our innocence, and, in ſome caſes, we ſhould be content to part even with our being itſelf to preſerve it.

Daphne fled from Apollo: She loſt her life but ſhe preſerved her honour. Her fair fame ſurvived her mortal body, and ſhe remained at once an emblem and a monument of virtue to poſterity.

She challenged reſpect even from him who was moſt diſappointed, and at the very time when he found himſelf foiled, he bore teſtimony to her honour and rewarded her glorious conſtancy.

Even they who ſeek to draw us into the ſnares of vice cannot help ſecretly applauding us when they ſee that, in ſpite of all their

arts,

arts, we still proceed in the paths of virtue. The harder the trial, the greater will be the reward to those who persevere.

But above all things it is necessary for us to fly from temptation. There are none who stand so strong but that it is possible they may fall: How unwise then is it for us to approach to the brink of a precipice, merely to try whether we can bear to look down from it with a steady eye. Those who seek a danger they may shun, deserve the consequences of their folly, when they meet it.

If we mean to triumph, let us take a different course. Let us fly from evil that we may overcome it; when human aid fails us, let us invoke Heaven itself to our assistance: so shall we be strengthened in our course, and in the end, by flying, attain the laurels of victory.

EMBLEM

EMBLEM XXXVI.

THE VANITY OF PLEASURE.

BEHOLD the beauty of yon' damask
  rose,
Joy of the eye, in gaudy pride it blows,
The setting sun shall see its bloom decay,
And all it boasted beauties fade away:
The envious thorns its fragnant leaves sur-
  round,
Protect the blossom, and th' unwary wound;
Pleasure must cost too dear when bought with
  pain:
The Rose shall wither, when the Thorns re-
  main.

 With cautious hand pluck the vain flow'r
  of joy,
Lest hidden evil should your soul annoy.

THE Rose, the pride of the garden is surrounded with sharp prickles, and he who is too eager to pluck the *former* stands a chance of being injured by the *latter*.

Yet after all, when the flower is obtained, in a few short hours, it must wither and die, its beauty is lost and it is despised and rejected by those who prized it before. The Thorns will remain even when the Rose is withered, and their sharpness ends only with their existence; be cautious then how you pluck the flower, and forget not the Thorn which guards it.

EVEN such, so transient, are the joys of life, which seem so inviting and court us, as it were, to taste them: they quickly wither and die, but are surrounded with Thorns whose smart is too often felt long after the sense of the pleasure is lost and extinguished.

Yet neither virtue nor prudence declare against the moderate enjoyment of the pleasures

sures of life; but we are admonished not to be too eager in our pursuit of them, lest we injure our health, our fortune, our reputation, or which is still worse, our virtue.

The difference between a moderate man, and one who pursues after pleasures to an extreme is thus beautifully described by the poet: where he says that

" ----Eager *this* its object would devour;
" *That* taste the honey, but not wound the flow'r.

And he who is in such haste after enjoyment, is likely to wound himself also, at the same time that his eagerness takes off from the relish he would otherwise have for the acquisition he has been at so much pains to obtain.

Learn then to set no more than a due value on the things of this world; be not overhasty to gain them, and when you possess them be moderate in your enjoyment; so shall
you

you be gratified with the beauty of the Rose, without wounding yourself with its Thorns; so shall you enjoy the honey of pleasure, while you avoid the sting and venom of remorse.

EMBLEM

EMBLEM XXXVII.

Of the Improvement of Life.

TIME's an hand's-breadth; 'tis a tale;
   'Tis a veffel under fail;
'Tis an eagle in its way,
Darting down upon its prey;
'Tis an arrow in its flight,
Mocking the purfuing fight;
'Tis a fhort liv'd fading flow'r;
'Tis a rainbow on a fhow'r;
'Tis a momentary ray,
Smiling in a winter's day;
'Tis a torrent's rapid ftream;
'Tis a fhadow; 'tis a dream;
'Tis the clofing watch of night,
Dying at the rifing light;
'Tis a bubble; 'tis a figh:---
Be prepar'd, O Man! to die.

TIME

TIME is the great destroyer of all things. There is nothing in this world which must not sooner or later submit to his stroke, none so strong as to resist, so cunning as to evade his power.

Yet this great destroyer steals on us, as it were, unperceived: The Days, the Months, the Years roll on: We content ourselves with saying "Time passes" without considering that *our* time also passes with it, and that every moment brings us nearer to eternity.

How much more praise-worthy would it be to mark each day of our existence with some act of religion or virtue, the remembrance of which might live when we ourselves are departed, and make our memory dear to the good, and our deeds approved by Heaven.

Titus Vespasian, Emperor of Rome, (though a heathen) was a man of so good a disposition, that recollecting one night as he sat at supper he had not done one good action that day, he cried out " Friends I have lost a day."---

This

This prince was furnamed by his people *The Delight of Mankind,*.---Happy are they who know fo well the value of Time, and make fo good an ufe of it.

HOW many are there amongft us who are for ever exclaiming againft the fhortnefs of life, and yet are not afhamed with the fame breath to complain, that their Time hangs heavy on their hands, and that they know not how to employ it?

But what an idle complaint is this, when we confider that there cannot be any perfon in any ftation of life whatfoever, who has not an opportunity of fpending his days in the exercife of fomething that is inftructive or ufeful to himfelf or others?---" Go to the Ant thou fluggard! Confider her ways, and be wife!"---Nor is the ufeful employment of Time confined to thofe only who muft get their bread by the fweat of their brow. Every good and wife man, however greatly he may be exalted by fortune above his fellow-creatures, will find that he may use his Time to the Glory of God, the service of his friends and country, or in some way that may be beneficial to society. And he who attends to the social duties of mankind, and is willing to read the great Book of Nature, which God hath set open for his instruction needs never chide the lagging hours, on the one hand, since he will know how to employ them well, nor complain of the shortness of human life, on the other hand, when he has an assurance that to the righteous man the end of *Time* is the beginning of an happy *Eternity*.

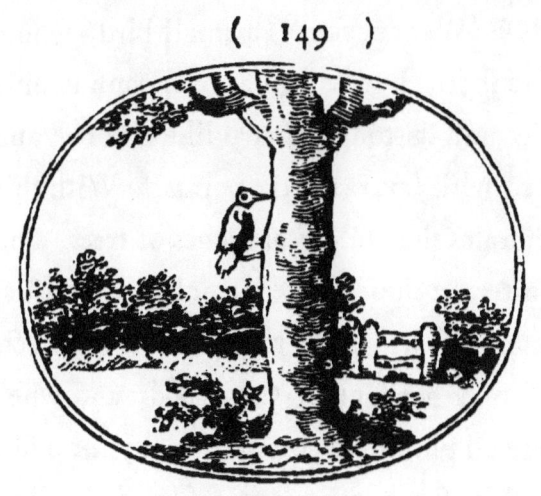

EMBLEM XXXVIII.

OF INDUSTRY.

WITH what hard toil, with what un-
ceasing cares,
The Woodpecker his scanty meat prepares,
Tho' small the feast that must reward his
pains,
Sweet is that meal which honest labour gains.

Be frugal, be industrious, if you're wise,
The way to plenty through these maxims lies.
The Idle to ill stars ascribe their state,
But Fools make fortune and deserve their Fate.

THE Woodpecker is a small bird, whose legs are short, but its bill is of a considerable length, and its tongue sharp like a horn, and fortified with several little points. With this it perforates the hollow branches of trees, and then utters a loud cry, not unlike a whistle, the intent of which is to disturb any insects which may harbour in the wood, and when they are all put into a commotion, by the assistance of its sharp tongue it easily catches and devours them.

So much pains does this bird take to come at a few minute reptiles which Nature has ordained for its prey, and on which alone, inconsiderable as they seem, it is destined to subsist----

A true pattern of industry, and an example of perseverance, which man need not be ashamed to copy; as the idle may learn an useful lesson from the labours of this little animal.

A S

AS idleness is generally the root of mischief, so is an honest industry the source of the most laudable and ingenious undertakings.

It is to this principle chiefly that we owe those arts and manufactures which at this day flourish amongst us, and which add to the convenience and grandeur of the great, while they subsist numbers of the lower class of people, who without them must be reduced to a starving condition, or have recourse to begging, in order to procure a subsistance.

In countries where such arts and manufactures are encouraged, though it is certain that nobody can guard against sickness or other accidents, yet, in general, all ranks of men are enabled to get an honest livelihood, by a proper degree of industry:—but some prefer a life of idleness to exerting their talents for the benefit of themselves and others; yet these are ever crying out upon their ill fortune, which indeed is of their own making, and, while they refuse to earn their bread, complain they *cannot procure it.* Such may learn a lesson of perseverance from this emblem, Let them put their shoulders to the wheel and Hercules will help them to lift their carriage out of the mire.

If you seek the blessings of Fortune strive by unremitted labour to attain them.---Deserve the bread you eat, and leave the rest to Heaven.

EMBLEM

EMBLEM XXXIX.

Of Evil and its Punishment.

WHILE the sweet nightingale chaunts
    forth her lays,
Her warbling throat the hidden nest betrays,
Eager to seize it, hastes the thoughtless boy,
And all the mother's comfort to destroy;
When lo! the faithless branch in pieces broke,
His limbs are shatter'd with the dreadful
    stroke

  So, when we seek some dear-priz'd joy to
    gain
And buy *our* pleasure with *another's* pain,
Our slipp'ry steps to evil are betray'd
We fall unpity'd in the snare we made.

THE sweet-warbling nightingale chears the silent plains with her melodious song;—the answering woods repeat the harmonious trillings of her voice; when lo! the wanton boy, guided by the sound draws near; he listens a while, and soon discovers whence it comes. Eager for the prize he hastens to rob the mother bird of her nest; but as he climbs the lofty tree, the bough that bears his unlucky weight gives way, and throws him on the ground. He mourns his fall with tears, and is at once disabled and discouraged from his enterprize.

This bird (says the fable) was once a Philomela, the daughter of Pandion, King of Athens. She was abused by Tereus King of Thrace who had married her sister. This tyrant afterwards deprived her of her tongue, that she might not tell her griefs. But she found her way to his court, and worked the story in a sampler, which she presented to her sister Procne, who revenged her husband's barbarity by killing the son she had by him—Philomela, after this, being pursued by him

who

who threatened her for being concerned in his death, took wing, and was changed into a nightingale, which, mindful of its former state, continues ever to sing mournful notes in solitary places.

THEY who seek their own good at the expence of that of others often meet with a bitter difappoinment, and lament too late the evils which themfelves have occafioned.

If every man would do to others as he would wifh to be done by, evil would be banifhed from the world, peace and righteoufnefs would flourifh, man would draw nearer to the Divine Nature, and earth would be a reprefentation of Heaven.

But while people will follow their own evil inclinations, they have no right to complain of the ills they fuftain : fince, as virtue makes happinefs, vice muft at one time or another, end in mifery.

In

In particular, when a man endeavours by force or fraud to prejudice his neighbour, if the evil fhould recoil upon himfelf, its weight is double, becaufe he is confcious he deferved it. Like the boy in the Emblem, he may be faid to be the author of his own evil; *becaufe he laid a fnare for others and is fallen into the midſt of it himſelf*, therefore his fate is unlamented, and in the day of his trouble there fhall be none to affift him.

EMBLEM XL.

OF VAIN GLORY.

BEHOLD that silly bird, how proudly vain,
Of the bright colours of his gaudy train!
Ev'n to a proverb grown his idle pride
By outward shew alone in worth supply'd,
For no harmonious sound, no chearful note,
Must ever issue from that hideous throat,
Nor of the hundred eyes that grace his tail,
Can one for sight, or real use avail.

O son of vanity be wise in time!
Apply the moral of this homely rhyme,
To *real worth* alone should praise be giv'n,
And *real worth* inherits it from Heav'n.

JUNO

JUNO, says the fable, having set Argus who had 100 eyes to guard and torment the damsel Iö who was transformed into a young heifer, Hermes (or Mercury) commissioned by Jupiter, descended from Heaven to deliver her.

He found Argus busily employed about his charge, but sitting down by him began to tell him stories, by virtue of which, and of his charming rod he at length lulled all his hundred eyes to sleep; which being done, he slew him by cutting off his head.---On which Juno took the eyes of her servant and placed them in the tail of the **Peacock**, a bird esteemed sacred to her who was in a great measure the Goddess of Pride and Splendour.——So far Ovid.—As to the Peacock it is a bird known in most countries for its fine plumage, which indeed seems to be all it has to boast of; for as to its voice, it is a most frightful one, and the flesh of it, though a rarity, is generally own'd to have no very delicate flavour. The pride this bird takes in its plumage and the ill tone of its voice are both become equally

pro-

proverbs, and it is worth while to obferve that the former circumftance has ferved to make the latter more remarkable.

LIKE the proud Peacock is the fon of vanity—and furely it is more ridiculous in a rational creature to indulge this pride than in an unreafoning animal.

But what is the vain glorious man proud of---his drefs?---Surely the Peacock has more reafon to be proud of what nature gave her than man of that covering for which, at beft, he is obliged to the brutes or to the vegetable creation.

Is it of the beauties of his perfon that he is vain. Let him confider how fhortly ficknefs or accident may, how certainly old age *muft*, if he attains it, deprive him of thofe. Let him confider likewife, at beft, how worthlefs they are without mental qualifications. A fine houfe unfurnifhed is but an uncomfortable dwelling.

Yet to be vain of great talents is abfurd---Whatever men poffeffes comes from Heaven; to Heaven then let him give the glory, and always remember that the wifeft of men are far from the proudeft, according to thofe lines of the poet.

> ————What is it to be WISE?
> " 'Tis but to know what LITTLE's to be known,
> " To *see* all *other's* faults, and *feel* our own.

In fhort, let us argue the matter how we will, every fenfible perfon muft be convinced by reafon that nothing is fo odious as PRIDE, nothing fo childifh as VAIN GLORY.

EMBLEM XLI.
Of Applause.

FAME! that strange pow'r which ev'ry moment grows:
"And gather strength and vigour as she goes,
"First small with fear she swells to wondrous size,
"And stalks on earth, or tow'rs above the skies,
"Beneath her various plumes she ever bears,
"A thousand piercing eyes and list'ning ears,
"And with a thousand mouths and babbling tongues appears."
 Lo! to this goddess ev'ry mortal bends,
And still from pole to pole her tyrant-reign extends.
Wisdom and virtue will for ever claim
The deathless honours of an honest Fame,
Where these are wanting weak is he who draws
His fund of glory from a vain applause.

FAME,

FAME, as represented in the Emblem, was one of the deities of the ancients, who described her as a monstrous figure, and reported her to be the daughter of the giant Enceladus, who warred with Jupiter. They say that *Terra* or the earth being angry with the gods for having destroyed her offspring, brought forth this last of monsters, which she sent into the world to publish their excesses.

Thus far the fable---Of this fictitious Being, the poets have given the most lofty and extraordinary descriptions---Though all seem to have agreed that she did not always strictly confine herself to truth nor reward people according to their deserts.

――――Some she disgrac'd, and some with honours crown'd,
Unlike successes equal merits found :
Thus her blind sister fickle Fortune reigns,
And, undiscerning, scatters crowns and chains.

But it needs not be wondered at, that the heathens whose supreme Jupiter was defective should

should suppose all the subservent deities to be imperfect.---

---

THE love of FAME is justly sty'd the universal passion---All men seem possessed of it;---but in their pursuit of applause, as in that of happiness, it falls out that various people take different roads to attain it.

In the desire itself there is certainly nothing amiss; it is implanted in our Nature as an incentive to virtue and, doubtless, to this we owe many of the best and greatest actions which have been performed;---if it were taken away, the world would become worse than it is, as the force of example in the cause of virtue would be far less prevalent.

But, as there is an excess and likewise a perversion of all things; so it is in regard to Fame: Men often mistake glaring characters for *virtuous* ones, and hence has arose the false glory which has been too often attributed to the destroyers of mankind This is the perversion of Fame.---An excess in courting

ing her favours is also an abuse too frequent.
---But these are no arguments against the glorious emulation in the minds of the good to excel in wisdom and virtue: where these are not the ends designed, all applause is adulation, and Fame an empty bubble; so that we may well conclude

>"All praise is foreign but of true desert,
>Plays round the head, but comes not near the heart."

EMBLEM

EMBLEM XLII.

Of Oppression.

FROM airy heights the rav'nous bird survey,
With matchless swiftness darting on her prey,
The helpless, struggling victim strives in vain
From such a foe its freedom to regain,
Proudly secure. she skims the skies along,
And hastens home to feed her hungry young;
But when the wily Serpent's strength she tries,
And strives to bear aloft her scaly prize,
At once the victor with the vanquish'd dies.

Beware of vice with lawless might combin'd:
All ills are easy to a wicked mind,
But if an useful lesson you would prove,
Be wise as Serpents, harmless as the dove.

THE Eagle, as we have already obferved is one of the ftrongeft of the feathered kind;---It is likewife the moft voracious---It has been faid of the lion that he will not prey upon carcaffes; but the contrary is true of the Eagle, which, notwithftanding, is no lefs fierce in its attacks upon living animals---Birds, Beafts, and even Serpents are its prey; and if the dove falls often a victim to this feathered tyrant, the hare with all its fwiftnefs cannot always efcape its pounces: ftooping, as it were from the clouds the deftroyer feizes on the timorous creature, and carries her off with incredible fwiftnefs---But when the Eagle and the Serpent meet the combat is longer and more doubtful, for though borne through the air by a force fuperior to his own, the wily reptile ftruggling curls his angry fpires, and often, even in that fituation, mortally

tally wounds his conqueror; so that he either escapes, or both fall down dead together. Thus his cunning serves either to deliver or revenge him, while the poor innocent hare falls an easy victim to the great oppressor.---

———————

IT is thus that unsuspecting innocence is often lost and ruined: It is thus that guilty greatness triumphs in destruction. Virtue alone cannot always be safe from the danger of slander or oppression.----Caution is therefore a good companion, and a necessary guard to keep us from the force or fraud of arbitrary or designing men.

It is a great mistake of those who suppose Prudence to be incompetible with Goodness-- A low and vicious cunning may indeed justly be deemed so; but some of the most virtuous characters that have graced humanity, have

also

also been the most remarkable for wisdom, which has been conspicuous in all their conduct even to the end of their days, and transmitted in their writings to posterity.

Follow their example; follow the precepts of ONE greater than them. Adopt the Serpent's wisdom, though you avoid being tainted with his guile, lest like the timerous hare you become an easy prey to the wicked, because they apprehend they have nothing to fear from you, and that you are not endued with prudence enough to escape them.

EMBLEM

EMBLEM XLII.
Of the Vanity of Self-Love.

THE fond Narcissus in the chrystal flood,
His own fair form with secret pleasure view'd,
Of his own face enamoured oft retires,
When the warm sun darts forth meridian fires,
To the clear fountain, there enraptur'd lies,
In vain to catch the fleeting shadow tries,
And smit with hopeless love despairing dies.
The Theban nymphs a rustic tomb prepare,
Rend their fair garments, tear their golden hair:
But to a flow'r transform'd the corpse remains,
Which still his name and memory sustains.

The self-admiring youth whose weake mind,
Is still to childish vanity inclin'd,
Will find too late by the vain shew betray'd,
He courts indeed *the shadow of a shade*.

NARCISSUS, according to Ovid, was a beautiful youth, who delighted in hunting, and was beloved by Eccho, then a nymph. However, he equally flighted her and all his admirers, at length viewing his own face in a fountain, fell in love with himself, and constantly reforted to the ftream to court his own fhadow in the water.

But when he perceiv'd the beautiful form to retire as often as he withdrew, and to mock his purfuit when he ftretched out his arms to embrace it, he fell into the greateft agonies of paffion, and with vain prayers invoked the infubftantial form.

Tho' convinc'd at laft, of his miftake, and affured that the figure he faw was only the reflexion of himfelf, he yet could not conquer his unhappy paffion, but ftill continued to pine with a prepofterous love of his own perfon—Thus his form wafted, his beauty decayed, and the breath of life at laft forfook him; but when his body was fought for to be interred, in its ftead they found a flower
which

which still retains his name, and perpetuates his memory.

Such is the story, in which the fabulist seems to have included a very striking moral against Vanity and Self-Love, which is worthy of surviving to future ages, and being handed down to posterity.

THERE is not a greater vanity or folly than those of Self-love and Self-admiration; he who inclines to them will court a vain shadow and will ever like the youth in the fable, find himself disappointed.

And besides, what tribute of applause, what share of honest fame can he expect to receive at the hands of others, who is ever employed in admiring his own person, and sounding forth his own praises?

But it happens to too many persons of weak minds, as it did to Narcissus, that they suffer themselves to be led away with such vanities before they know that they are possessed by them and, are far gone in the intoxication of

Self-love before they are aware of it—The ill-habit, strengthened by custom thus grows too powerful for their reason, and the consequence is that they often become the authors of their own misfortunes only by loving themselves too well.

Reflect on this and prevent the growing evil; consider these things and be wise; for he who is too proud of himself is not in the road to success, *but he that humbleth himself shall be exalted.*

EMBLEM

(173)

EMBLEM XLIV.

Of the Danger of Greatness.

WITH dreadful force, the lofty tree of Jove,
Is struck and rent by lightning from above,
Mossy and old its shiver'd trunk appears,
The growth of ages, yet unhurt by years;
Long had it flourish'd and with stately pride,
The utmost force of fighting winds defy'd.
But yet in dust its honours stretch'd at last,
In dreadful ruin by th' æthereal blast;
While the low shrub, in far more humble state,
Unknown to Greatness, stands secure from fate.

Would you security and peace obtain?
Contented in a private state remain.

THE Oak is one of the ſtrongeſt trees of the foreſt. It is ſaid to be a century in growing, to continue a century in perfection, and to be a century more in decaying---However this account may be exaggerated, yet it is certain that it flouriſhes a long time, of which we have many inſtances in this land---This tree is generally found to reſiſt the greateſt tempeſts, except when, as in the Emblem, it is ſtruck by lightning, which ſometimes cleaves it to the ground.

The Oak was eſteemed ſacred among the Romans---It ſtood at Cæſar's gate, together with the laurel; which was held in high veneration; and they even pretended to have ſome which delivered oracles---The ancient Britons, the firſt inhabitants of theſe iſlands, alſo held it ſacred, as they alſo did Miſletoe, and ſome of their Druids or Prieſts are ſaid to have delivered their lectures on the religion

of

of their country, from the spreading branches of this lofty tree.

———

THIS Emblem is well adapted to represent the dangers generally inseparable from greatness, and the security of a private and obscure station. To be great is to be set as a mark for all the shafts of misfortune, to be exposed to all the storms of adverse Fate, which generally delights in sporting with persons in exalted stations. To live in an humble situation is the most likely way to escape tempests on the troubled sea of life, and to get safe at last into the harbour of peace and tranquility.

That man is happiest who having little to fear, and much to hope, and can set a just bound to his wishes, and thereby never reduce himself, by aspiring at grandeur, to the contrary situation. Content dwells not with

with power, neither is Security the child of wealth and honours: If thou wouldst taste the serene joys of life, fly far from greatness, and make thy abode with the daughter of simplicity.

EMBLEM

EMBLEM XLV.

OF HEAVENLY LOVE.

THE tender Pelican with ceaseless cares,
    Protects her young ones and their food
        prepares,
From her own breast the nourishment proceeds,
With which, as with her blood, her brood
    she feeds:
Emblem of Heavn's supernal graces known,
And parents love to dearest children shewn.

    To God above and to your friends below,
Still let your breast with zeal and duty glow:
Much to your parents, more to heav'n you
    owe.

THE Pelican is a bird whofe name is well enough known to moſt people. It has given rife to many ſtrange ſtories, the principal of which is, that of its feeding its young with its blood, which, however, upon examination, has not proved to be true. But this creature has a bag or pouch in which it puts proviſion to fupply their wants, and doubtlefs the manner of the female's taking it from that repoſitory appeared to the firſt obfervers of it, as if fhe had made an opening in her breaſt, and nouriſhed them with their blood; and from thence occaſion has been taken to make it a fymbol of Chriſtianity——— However, as the matter really ſtands, the Pelican may with great propriety be eſteemed as an Emblem of the cares of Heaven and our parents, to which at all times in general, but

more

more particularly in youth, we are so highly indebted for the preservation of our Being, and which consequently claim from us the sincerest returns of gratitude and love.

IN this Emblem is expressed the state of dependance we are in, on the one hand, and the great goodness of God on the other, who equally supplies our temporal and our spiritual wants, and who sent his only Son to be a propitiation for our sins, who as it were nourished us with his blood, and *by whose stripes we are healed.*——The Pelican indeed if she had granted this supply from her own vitals would have done it only to her brood; but the great Author of our salvation did this for wicked offenders, he died even for his

greatest

greatest enemies, and bore our sins that he might be made righteousness for us, and that we might proceed from grace to grace till at last we were made heirs of his glorious inheritance.

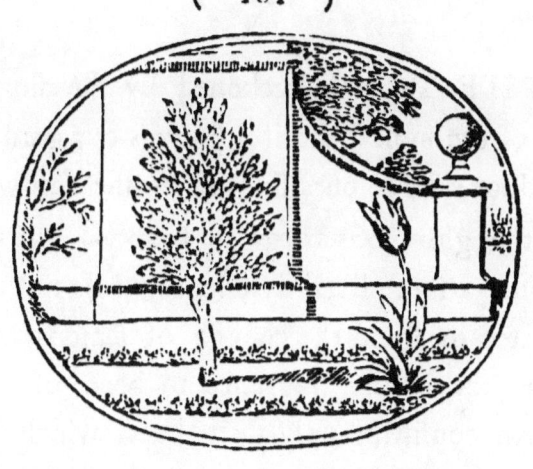

EMBLEM XLVI.

Of False Appearances.

SEE the gay Tulip dipp'd in various dyes,
  Blooms in full pride beneath the vernal
    skies;
But when the wintry clouds deform the year,
How faded will that beauteous form appear!
Not so the Myrtle, deck'd in chearful green,
The humble plant among the flow'rs is seen;
What tho' it boast no varied colours bright,
That drink Sol's radiance or reflect his light;
Yet ever green and fragrant it remains,
Nor change of seasons, nor of time sustains.

  Emblem of real worth, whose gloomiest hour
Transcends the blaze of pomp, excels the
    pride of pow'r.

THE Tulip is reckoned by the florists one of the most beautiful flowers our gardens produce; its colours shining in the sun with all the glow of variegated beauty---But this is only a short-lived excellence; it is not calculated to stand the change of seasons, neither has it any fragrance to boast of. Its worth consisting only in its hues, which fading, it is passed by unregarded, because it has nothing intrinsic to recommend it.

But the Myrtle disperses a sweet fragrance round about it, and though it produces no various coloured flowers to glitter in the sunbeams, yet it always preserves Nature's own hue, and flourishing an ever-green through the year, is admired for its constancy. that renders it preferable to all those gaudy tints of the Tulip which only bloom to fade and are equally devoid of fragrance as they are of continuance.

WE are not always to trust to appearances, nor to conclude on the merit of persons or the

the worth of things from their outward form and shew, since there is nothing more common in the world than for people to affect being what they are not, and those often make the greatest shew of worth, who have in reality, the least to recommend them.

Not only pomp and splendour, wit and talents, but even virtue and religion are affected, by such as are far from being possessed of either; and he who is led away by the dazzling appearance in either of these cases prefers the Tulip to the Myrtle, and must expect to succeed accordingly.

Be not therefore hasty in your determinations in regard to men or things; but *try all things, and hold fast that which is best*. Trust not merely to the boast of peoples abilities, nor the warmth of their professions to serve you, lest you be taken merely with the wind of words, and deserted in time of adversity.

Above all, be careful how you are deceived by an affectation of sanctity of manners, which is too often used as a cloak for evil, and

and a snare to delude the unwary into vice.---
Be more attentive to deeds than words, and do not make connexions too hastily lest you repent them at leisure.------

Take care to be well acquainted with the disposition of men; *for by their fruits you shall know them*; and remember that those who make the greatest professions are seldom the most friendly, and that constancy and sincerity are the inseparable companions of virtue and merit.

EMBLEM

EMBLEM XLVII.

Of the Frailty of Sublunary Things.

THE lofty pile that rear'd its head so high,
Aspiring still and pointing to the sky,
The boast of ages, but their boast in vain:
O'erturn'd at last and levell'd with the plain.
So falls the pride of life; so worlds must fall,
And one long, last oblivion bury all.

Time conquers all things! Would you Time survive,
Be good, and in your virtuous actions live,
For virtue shall resist the tyrant's sway,
And bloom, and flourish in eternal day.

THUS

THUS must the most lofty and the strongest edifices decay! if they escape storms, tempests, and earthquakes, yet must they yield at last to Time and their glories be buried in the dust.

Pyramids are justly reckoned the greatest instances of the folly and vanity of mankind.---The use for which those famous ones in Egypt were erected was only for their kings to be interred in.----And it is even said by some writers that a monarch who had built one of them for this purpose, was not after death suffered to be laid in this his monument because he had been a great tyrant in life; and, amongst other accusations brought against him, was that of having caused a number of innocent men to lose their lives in executing this magnificent plan;---a striking instance of the vanity of men's desires, who often defeat by their vices and follies those ends they are prompted to pursue, by their ambition,

TAKE a view of the ruins of antiquity, and remember O man, the frail state of thy mortality!---Art thou rich and great, is thy name known throughout the world, and do thy lofty buildings aspire to the clouds? Yet a little while, and thou shalt sink in dust. Thy edifices and thy monuments too must at length decay and leave no traces behind them.

Where now is Babylon? Where is the seat of Solomon? Where is wise Athens? and where ancient Rome, the mistress of the world? Where are those mighty cities once so famous upon earth?---Of some there is not left even a stone upon a stone, and others are remembered only in their ruins.

> E'en as an insubstantial pageant faded
>   The cloud-capt tow'rs, the gorgeous palaces,
>   The solemn temples, the great globe itself;
>   Yea, all which it inherit, shall dissolve,
>   And like the baseless fabric of a vision
>   Leave not a wreck behind.

Be

Be affured then, O man, who gloriest in thy ftrength and might that there is nothing folid but peace of mind, nothing permanent but virtue: She alone fhall laft through the ages and grow brighter through the endlefs fucceffion of Eternity.

INDEX.

	Emb.	Page
A		
Ambition	XXVIII	109
Applause	XLI	151
B		
Brotherly Love	XI	41
C		
Constant Affection	VII	25
Confidence	VIII	29
Cares of Grandeur	X	37
Changes of Human Affairs	XXXII	125
Chastity	XXXV	137

Deceit

                                      Emb.   Page
                    D
Deceit   -   -   -   XVII   165
Danger of Temptation   -   XXV   97
——— of Greatness   -   XLIV   173

                    E
Education   -   -   -   XXI   81
Evil Principle (of resisting)   XXII   85
Evil (its Punishment)   - XXXIX   153

                    F
Filial Duty and Affection   -   I   1
Fidelity   -   -   -   IV   13
False Friendship   -   -   -   XX   77
Fortitude   -   -   -   XXIII   89
False Appearances   -   -   XLVI   181
Frailty of sublunary Things   XLVII   185

                    G
Guilt   --   --   -   VI   21

                    H
Human Grandeur   --   --   XIII   49

                                      Instability

	Emb.	Page
I		
Instability - - -	XV	57
Improvement - - -	XVI	61
Inordinate Desire - -	XVIII	69
Industry -- --	XXXVIII	129
L		
Love, (heavenly) - -	XLV	175
O		
Oppression ———	XLII	165
P		
Pleasure (its Danger) --	III	9
Purity - - -	V	17
Perseverance - -	XXVI	101
Punishment of the Selfish	XXX	117
Precipitation - -	XXXI	121
Passion - -	XXXIV	133
Pleasure (its Vanity) -	XXXVI	141
S		
Silence - - -	II	5
Self-Denial (its Use) -	XXIV	93
Snares of Vice -	XXXIII	129

Temperance

		Emb.	Page
T			
Temperance	- -	XIX	73
Time	- -	XXXVII	145
V			
Use of Time	- -	XII	45
Vain Pursuits	--	XXVII	105
Vice (its Reward)	-	XXIX	113
Vain Glory	- -	XL	147
Vanity of Self-Love	-	XLIII	169
W			
Wisdom	- -	XIV	53
Z			
Zeal towards GOD	-	IX	33

www.ingramcontent.com/pod-product-compliance
Lightning Source LLC
Chambersburg PA
CBHW020913230426
43666CB00008B/1443